freeing, convicting, and empowering biblical perspectives on what it means to walk with kids toward Jesus. Careful, compassionate, and realistic, this book helps readers see that through Jesus, they truly can raise disciples at home."

—**Bethany McIlrath**, author of the Abigail series and kids ministry volunteer

"I hoped to learn a thing or two about discipling my four children by reading *Raising Disciples at Home*. That happened. Big time. But I also felt seen and cared for as a parent, with one refreshing light bulb moment after another. This is the most insightful book for parents I have read in ages, but also the most delightful! To achieve both is hard to do, but Chris Ammen has written a page-turner. I devoured it! I'd encourage you to do the same."

—**Amber Lia,** bestselling co-author of *Triggers*

"Sit down, read *Raising Disciples at Home*, and take a deep breath of grace and encouragement. Parenting can be hard. Chris Ammen reminds readers that while growth *is* always possible, it is the magnificent love of God for us parents that *makes it* possible. Filled with practical tools and biblical wisdom, this book guides parents on a journey toward becoming more loving and intentional in their parenting. It's a gift for anyone wishing to parent from a place of grace rather than guilt."

—**Benjie Slaton**, lead pastor of Grace+Peace Church in Chattanooga, Tennessee

"*Raising Disciples at Home* is a powerful rem.
pleship is not about formulas or rigid program.
faithfully putting your kids where God is working
ing him to do what only he can do. With wit and w
this book invites parents to release the pressure of being
fect' and instead embrace the beautiful truth that it's G.
who molds our children's hearts. A refreshing and necessary
read for any parent longing to raise kids who love Jesus."

—**Jerrad Lopes**, founder of Dad Tired

"With wisdom and disarming humor, Chris has brought us
the book every Christian parent needs. This book empowers
parents to share their faith with their kids while simultaneously setting them free from the overwhelming pressure of
trying to do the impossible—parenting perfectly and saving
our children's souls by our own strength. Chris's call to make
disciples in our homes is one of the most important aspects
of Christian parenting and one that desperately needs the
help that Chris has laid out for us here."

—**Adam Griffin**, lead pastor of Eastside Community Church in
Dallas, Texas, host of *The Family Discipleship Podcast*,
and author of several books and resources for families

"Reliance on Jesus may not sound complicated enough to
be a thoughtful, practical plan for discipling kids, but Chris
Ammen shows it is. In *Raising Disciples at Home*, he offers

Raising Disciples at Home

Chris Ammen

HARVEST HOUSE PUBLISHERS
EUGENE, OREGON

To my bride, Sarah.

Each day you become more beautiful to me.

I know Luke 20:35 is good news, and even still,
it makes me more than a little sad.

Contents

Introduction

W e need a Mountain Dew in here!" the nurse called as she administered an epidural to my eight-centimeters-dilated wife.

"I don't need a Mountain Dew!" Sarah replied in the way only someone twelve hours deep in sleep-deprived labor can.

She was right. The Mountain Dew was not for her. It was for me.

Within minutes of my wife's first contractions the previous day, my stomach tied itself in knots. I've never experienced anything like it. I could barely stand up straight. By the time Sarah told me we needed to go to the hospital, the most empathetic response I could muster was, "Can I lay down for thirty minutes before we go?"

You can imagine how well that was received.

Once settled in the delivery room, my wife labored epidural-free and with little support from me. I spent the next six hours either lying in a recliner watching reruns of *The Office* to take my mind off the pain or emptying my stomach of the previous night's dinner. An outside observer may have second-guessed who the real patient was.

And now, at the moment my wife would finally get some relief, I had gone white as a ghost, on the verge of passing out.

(We are still married, for those wondering.)

What I now know is that I didn't have food poisoning, a stomach bug, or the flu. Instead, I was experiencing the first of what has become an eleven-year battle with panic attacks. Something in my body knew the birth of our first child was a big deal. Life as I knew it was about to change. I couldn't control it. I couldn't run away from it. Another human would soon depend on me for life. I wasn't exactly sure I was ready. I'm still not. We have four kids now.

Raising kids is a terrifying prospect. Don't listen to anyone who tells you it's easy. It's not. Nobody has this parenting thing figured out. As I loaded our child in the car a few days after my Mountain Dew experience, I had the unmistakable feeling that I was stealing him from the hospital. He really belonged to the nurses, and we would bring him back in a few hours. He was just a loaner baby. Nobody would actually trust me with a real live person. But there he was, day after day, growing up in our home.

Now, here's the thing nobody tells you at baby showers: The first year is all the easy stuff. If you are in the first year as you read this, I know it does not feel that way. You are physically exhausted and can no longer use the bathroom in peace and quiet. Take whatever comfort you can from this…it only gets harder.

One day soon, your child will have words and opinions. Your cute, saggy-diapered beauty queen will confront you about your sin. Your precious little boy will become an entitled troublemaker. You can't stop it. It's like one of the laws of nature or something.

And yet, God has asked you (*yes, you*) to lead your children to Jesus. This is what I'll refer to in this book as *discipleship*. This word may be familiar to you. If it is, you likely attach it to the concept of teaching your children about sin, repentance, and salvation. You may exclusively see discipleship as a church or parachurch activity like Sunday school or small groups. While these are part of discipleship, those ideas, activities, and strategies don't present a complete picture of the role that God and parents play in a child's spiritual formation.

As much as you may try to do all the right things, there is a limit to your influence as a parent. If you are new to parenting, allow me to pull the curtain back on how discipleship will go for you. You will do your best to train your children in the way they should go, and everything in their bodies and hearts will resist that training. You will make a great plan, you will execute it to perfection, and even still, your son or daughter will intentionally try to break you.

Before you close this book and return it to wherever you bought it from, please understand that this is the most loving thing I can possibly think to tell you. Your child will not cooperate with your discipleship. You are not ready for the task of raising disciples. You never will be. And *that* is the very best news you can hear.

In a world of gurus and advice columns, certainly there should be a manual for how to raise God-honoring children. Maybe you even picked up this book thinking it was like *Discipleship for Dummies*. It's not.

There is no formula, no curriculum, no reading plan, and no catechism that will make your kids into faithful followers of Jesus. That's not the way it works.

In fact, the Bible itself provides very little direct instruction on the mechanics of discipleship. We've already hinted at a few places it does, but let's look further: "Train up a child in the way he should go; even when he is old he will not depart from it" (Proverbs 22:6).

"*Train* them?" Thanks, King Solomon. Got it. Care to elaborate?

> You shall teach them diligently to your children, and shall talk of them when you sit in your house, and when you walk by the way, and when you lie down, and when you rise. You shall bind them as a sign on your hand, and they shall be as frontlets between your eyes. You shall write them on the doorposts of your house and on your gates (Deuteronomy 6:7-9).

Thank you, Moses. Teach. Talk. Write. Is that all you have for us? Bind them on my hand? Write them on my gates? I'm pretty sure the HOA will take issue with that.

The New Testament gives us a little more to go on. Luke 2 is a remarkable scene of a twelve-year-old Jesus learning from elders in Jerusalem. However, we have no record of Jesus's parents, Mary or Joseph, teaching him anything.

In 2 Timothy 1, Paul indicates that Timothy likely learned the faith from his mother and grandmother, but any discussion of how they passed it on is notably absent.

At this point, all my type A friends have simultaneously gone into mental paralysis. I know this drives you crazy. You want a concrete action plan, and yet the Bible won't give it to you.

But what I'm going to invite you to see in this book is that this lack of a plan is a gift. In fact, if the good news of the gospel is indeed good news, there are at least three freedoms we should experience as we disciple our children. We will circle back to each of these multiple times throughout this book.

Freedom #1: You are far less important than you think you are. God never puts you, the parent, at the center of your child's salvation. Hear that again— you are not the lynchpin of your child's journey of discipleship. *God is*. In the best of scenarios, you are merely able to encourage what God is already doing in your child's life. In most cases, we might say, the best parents can do is to lead their children to the places God has promised to work and then get out of the way. As much as you want your children to know God, he is infinitely more invested in knowing them.

Freedom #2: You can make mistakes. Adam Grant, in his book *Hidden Potential: The Science of Achieving Greater Things*, writes that perfectionists get three things wrong: they obsess about silly and insignificant details, they avoid taking risks, and they don't learn from their mistakes.[1] The good news of the

---

1. Adam Grant, *Hidden Potential: The Science of Achieving Greater Things* (Penguin Publishing Group, 2023), 67.

kingdom of God is that we are free to try and fail, to try and learn, and to try and occasionally get it right. Even the best of parents, according to therapist Dan Allender, only "get it right" 50 percent of the time.

Freedom #3: You are far more important than you think you are. *Come again?* Doesn't that debunk Freedom #1? Not in the slightest. God's ordinary means of working in our lives is through the encouragement, generosity, and kindness of other people. It is no accident that you are your child's parent. You are the person for the job! God wants to work through you to bless your child. The freedom of this truth comes in the openhanded confession of "God, I do not know how to do this. I need you to show me."

On December 6, 2012, I desperately needed to hear these truths. Instead, I got a Mountain Dew. I want better for you. I want you to know the delight God takes in you as a person, see the beautiful ways he is at work in your children, and find the courage to come alongside them in the helpful ways God has appointed for you.

Now, let me couch everything I'm about to say in the rest of this book. I am a pastor, not a professional theologian. I am practical before I am theoretical. Those looking for the precision of a young whippersnapper fresh out of seminary may be disappointed. Instead, this book is a set of musings from a fellow parent about topics I have found helpful, even essential, when it comes to raising disciples in your home.

Maybe I'm a lot like you. Just a man in his early forties going through a midlife crisis, taking stock of his life, and seeing that he may have something of relative value to offer the world. I'm glad you're here. Maybe you'll find in this book a helpful conversation partner. Perhaps it will make you feel less alone in your journey.

Maybe you are like me fifteen years ago, starry-eyed at the prospect of raising children. The worst your children have done to you so far is pee in your face or run out in the street. They haven't yet looked you square in the eye and said, "I hate you!" and slammed the door in your face. Don't worry, it will happen to you too. Nobody faults you for your lack of humiliation. I'm glad you're here. This is the type of book I wish I had read in the "urine in my face" stage.

Maybe you are twenty-five years older than me. Most of life is in the rearview, and you may even have grandchildren of your own. Maybe you look back with regret on the ways you raised your children. Maybe you have fond memories and wish you could relive the "glory days." Perhaps some of the ideas in this book are ones you've never considered. Remember this—your last lap of the race might be your best lap. Your adult children and grandchildren still need you, just in different ways. I hope you are a part of a church with young families who desperately need your leadership. You may be on your last lap, and it is probably your most important.

Whatever your station in life, I hope you walk away from this book closer to Jesus. Whether you pick up any tips, tricks, or strategies is secondary. What your children need from you is a compelling example of what it means to follow Jesus. The only way for you to be that for your children is to draw near to him daily.

CHAPTER 1

What Is Discipleship?

The step into the situation where faith is possible is not an offer which we can make to Jesus, but always his gracious offer to us.

—Dietrich Bonhoeffer

I wasn't sure why we kept going to random people's homes, but we did. Sometimes on short notice. We didn't even really know them all that well. I was told to play in close proximity to their children for an hour or so. "Y'all are too far apart; can you play closer together? Try breathing on one another. If you see someone put a toy in their mouth, do your best to lick it as many times as possible. That's right—the more, the better."

These scenarios no longer exist with the advent of modern vaccines, but in the 1980s, they were all the rage. Pox parties. One family's children got the chicken pox, so the whole neighborhood rushed to their house to get their kids infected. The goal was to get the chicken pox as young as possible because then you would have immunity to it and your case was less likely to be severe.

The aim of these parties was not too dissimilar to the goal of discipleship. As Christian parents, we want to raise our children to love Jesus. And so we put them in the places where God is already at work, much like my mother put us in the places where we were likely to catch what we now know is an extremely dangerous virus. Thanks, Mom.

If you are a Christian parent, I know you want your children to walk with Jesus. You want them to love God with all their heart, mind, soul, and strength. If you hold these desires, however, you will face some of the most challenging headwinds the people of God have known for quite some time. Our culture is set on cultivating the values of autonomy, power, independence, gender fluidity, wealth, and sexual freedom. However, as external pressures have increased, many churches have become distracted. Functionally, some church leaders appear more concerned with live streams and stage design than the basic task of discipleship. Publishing houses, for their part, produce new and exciting resources as fast as they can, but it doesn't seem to move the needle of families drifting from the faith. The paradox is bewildering: Despite living in a time with more robust discipleship resources than any other time in human history, actual disciple-making is at an all-time low.

To make matters worse, among the deficiencies of the modern church are its understanding and practice of child discipleship. In our attempts to make things better, many church leaders have felt the solution is to provide neat and tidy definitions of discipleship and statistics we can measure and report back to the congregation. As a children's pastor, I have felt pressure over the years—both from other staff members and parents—to crystallize and quantify exactly what discipleship is. Rarely does it dawn on us that our need for precision and clarity around questions about discipleship is far more of a Western value than a biblical one.

In the modern West, we love definitions. If we can define it, we believe we can understand it, and if we understand it, we think we can control it. But that was not the world Jesus grew up in. Eastern cultures embrace mystery and uncertainty far more readily. Western versions of discipleship are often culturally appropriated expressions of what Jesus and his disciples experienced. This appropriation is not necessarily wrong, but it is worth our reflection so we can gain a deeper appreciation of what it means to be a disciple.

Take these definitions of discipleship, summarized from a random sampling of other parents on social media and within my local church context:

Discipleship is…

…teaching our children about God.

…having a relationship with God.

…going to church.

…growing in compassion for others.

…participating in a small group and/or Sunday school.

…learning to apply God's teaching to our lives.

…growing in the fruit of the Spirit.

…regularly reading your Bible and praying.

…building relationships with other Christians.

…loving God and loving your neighbor.

All these statements are true. They are all parts of discipleship. Our children ought to grow in love for God's word and prayer. They should build relationships with others. All these things are great, but our best appropriations of discipleship are only a fraction of the whole. It would be like asking you, "How do I throw a dinner party?" and you replying, "You put out silverware." True statement, but if you never send invitations, plan for, shop for, and prepare a meal—not to mention tidying your home to an artificial level of cleanliness—then you don't truly have a dinner party.

The same is true of discipleship. It's well past time for Christian parents to awaken to discipleship as Jesus knew it—the formation not simply of the mind or the will but of the whole person. We are complex creatures with motivations, experiences, deficiencies, passions, memories, liabilities, traumas, desires, talents, histories, and futures. Discipleship is nothing less than God molding and shaping the entirety of our personhood into his image as those who delight in him and bring him glory.

Did you catch that? Discipleship is primarily the activity of God, not the responsibility of man. In the words of Dietrich Bonhoeffer, "The step into the situation where faith is possible is not an offer which we can make to Jesus, but always his gracious offer to us."[1] Discipleship is the miraculous work God accomplishes through the work of the Holy Spirit. This is a fundamental yet profound paradigm shift.

You Are Not the Only Discipler of Your Children

As a children's pastor, I've known many parents who feel unqualified to be a disciple of Jesus, let alone disciple their own children. It's a shame. When I let myself think about it long enough, it saddens me. Well-intentioned churches all over the world tell parents a great lie, "You are the most important discipler of your children." When parents don't listen, they simply say it louder, more creatively, and more often. I used to tell the parents in my church this. No matter how many times I said it, and no matter how eloquently I communicated, these words didn't make them better parents. They didn't motivate them to be better disciple-makers. My words only made them feel more guilty.

To those parents, I am sorry. The primary burden of discipleship does not fall on your shoulders. Here's what I mean…

The call for parents to be the primary discipler of their children is typically drawn from one passage in Deuteronomy 6:

---

1. Dietrich Bonhoeffer, *The Cost of Discipleship* (Touchstone, 1995), 85.

> Hear, O Israel: The LORD our God, the LORD is one. You shall love the LORD your God with all your heart and with all your soul and with all your might. And these words that I command you today shall be on your heart. You shall teach them diligently to your children, and shall talk of them when you sit in your house, and when you walk by the way, and when you lie down, and when you rise. You shall bind them as a sign on your hand, and they shall be as frontlets between your eyes. You shall write them on the doorposts of your house and on your gates (verses 4-9).

Certainly, in the modern Western world, a parent's influence cannot be understated. The home, by virtue of time spent, is typically the primary place of spiritual formation for children. This investment of parents is good and commendable, but it is only a tangential application of Deuteronomy 6.

Notice who Deuteronomy 6 is addressed to: "Hear, O Israel." This was a corporate address so important it is repeated nearly word for word in Deuteronomy 11. These passages were written to the community of God's people: children, unmarried people, widows, parents, priests—the audience is everyone. The *you*s in this passage are misleading when translated into English, where the word is typically understood in the singular. Instead, the *you*s in the context of Deuteronomy 6 are more like *y'all*: "Y'all shall teach them diligently to your children."

In the cultural context of Deuteronomy 6, the act of raising, teaching, and training children was far more communal than it is today. Most often, generations of families lived together. Nobody lived on half-acre lots. Homes were clustered tightly together without windows and doors. Gathering food was a shared responsibility. Clean water was derived from a common source. You relied on others not simply for companionship but for survival. Communities depended on one another for everything, including the discipleship of children.

Today, we live in an entirely different world. It's nearly impossible to translate the experience of an ancient Near Eastern family to a modern American family. Just think of all the things that separate us now: privately-owned transportation, air-conditioned homes, work-from-home arrangements, indoor plumbing, and not just grocery stores…but grocery delivery.

Even technology—for as much as it connects us, also separates us. We keep people at arm's length by texting them instead of calling or even knocking on their door to ask a question. I can still remember the days when someone showing up at your door unannounced wasn't considered rude. It was just normal. Not anymore! Just yesterday, I texted my next-door neighbor before going over to ask to borrow butter, and we're actually really good friends.

Modernization has privatized nearly every aspect of life. And so it should come as no surprise that we've done much the same with discipleship. The modern assumption is that children are the property of their parents. The biblical assumption is that children belong first to God and then to the covenant community of God, of which their parents play an important but not isolated role. For instance, when Jesus was twelve, his parents accidentally left him behind in Jerusalem and didn't even realize he wasn't with them until they had traveled an entire day. Mary and Joseph simply supposed he was somewhere among the community of people traveling together.[2] Today, my wife and I don't pull out of the driveway until we do at least three head counts to make sure we actually have all four children.

Privatized discipleship minimizes the role of the church. It decouples children from the unique contributions of the community—teachers, coaches, mentors, neighbors, extended family, and friends. Biblical discipleship invites parents to keep a looser grip on our children while inviting other influential voices into their lives. We should avoid the error of romanticizing ancient Near Eastern culture. They had plenty of problems too. One thing is for certain, though—parents were not expected to be and do everything for their children.

---

2. Luke 2:44.

Deuteronomy 6 goes on to explain the purpose of "teaching our children diligently":

- "Take care lest you forget the LORD" (verse 12).
- "It is the LORD your God you shall fear. Him you shall serve and by his name you shall swear" (verse 13).
- "You shall diligently keep the commandments of the LORD your God" (verse 17).
- "You shall do what is right and good in the sight of the LORD" (verse 18).

The goal of all this teaching is so our children will know, remember, follow, and learn from God.

Parents, the primary role of discipleship belongs first and foremost to God. Believe it or not, he is more invested in your children than you are. He knew them, made them, and called them his own before you knew what their chubby cheeks looked like.[3] He knows everything about your child and works and wills for their good and his glory.[4] He alone began a good work in them and will bring it to completion.[5] Only from this posture of humility can we truly come alongside and trust the work God is already doing in our children. When we trust, we can stop trying to control outcomes and dictate timelines. When we trust, we decouple our self-worth from our children's spiritual development. It's not up to us. It's no longer a reflection on our "good" or "bad" parenting. The reality of the living God choosing to draw near to our children is a miracle no one can fathom and certainly no one can control.

---

3. Ephesians 1:4.
4. Philippians 2:13.
5. Philippians 1:6.

The Example of Paul and Timothy

The apostle Paul wrote two letters to a man named Timothy, whom he called his "beloved child." Timothy was not literally Paul's son, but he was as close to him as a son (they must have read Deuteronomy 6). Paul tells him in 2 Timothy 3,

> But as for you, continue in what you have learned and have firmly believed, knowing from whom you learned it and how from childhood you have been acquainted with the sacred writings, which are able to make you wise for salvation through faith in Christ Jesus. All Scripture is breathed out by God and profitable for teaching, for reproof, for correction, and for training in righteousness, that the man of God may be complete, equipped for every good work (verses 14-19).

Paul could have written a lot of things here, but he chose to highlight the work of God. The most important tool Timothy brought with him from childhood was being "acquainted with the sacred writings." What Timothy possessed in his knowledge of Scripture was nothing less than God himself because it is through the Scriptures that God has revealed himself to his children. The word of God is what taught, reproved, corrected, and trained Timothy. In other words, we might say that Timothy was discipled by God.

After God, the responsibility of discipleship belongs to the covenant community of believers known as the church, of which you, as your child's parent, play perhaps the most influential role. However, Paul knew that Timothy's momma was only part of the equation.

Paul reminds Timothy of the spiritual influences in his life: his grandmother, Lois, and his mother, Eunice.[6] Throughout 2 Timothy, Paul also recalls Timothy's other spiritual influences: himself, the household of Onesiphorus, and

---

6. 2 Timothy 1:5.

Prisca and Aquila, among others.[7] Timothy's mother is mentioned, but only alongside the good work of the covenant community of Lystra.

To some, it may feel like I'm overanalyzing discipleship or trying to ruffle feathers by being novel. I can assure you that neither of these is the case. Instead, I want to help families return to a place of sanity—a place where parents know the good limits of their power, influence, and capacities. From this place of humility we can ask for help and trust our church community to be for our children what we cannot be for them, and we can ask God to do what only he can do.

We can rest assured that God cares far more about our children than we do. Just look at the robust work of the Trinity in the work of disciple-making: The Father elects to save your children.[8] The Son willingly offers himself as the Savior and Mediator to redeem your children from the punishment of sin.[9] The Holy Spirit provides Christ with the gifts necessary to accomplish his saving work and also applies the benefits of Christ's work (regeneration, justification, sanctification, glorification, and so on) to those whom the Father gives to the Son.[10]

Parents, you can do none of those things. Yes, you love your children. Yes, you want them to know Jesus. But you are limited in ways God is not. Do not let your need for control allow your children to experience more of your liabilities than they do of God's grace.

Your job, as we will see in a moment, is simply to put your children in the places God has promised to work, where they can sit at his feet, walk with him, and learn from him. Then, you can step back, watch, pray, and marvel at the work God does in your child. This role is God's gracious news that you are merely a limited human with finite power. But, it is also a welcome for you to

---

7. 2 Timothy 1:13, 16; 4:19.
8. Ephesians 1:4.
9. Luke 22:29; Hebrews 10:5–7.
10. Luke 1:35; 3:21–22; 4:18; John 6:38–39; 17:4.

join in the process in the ways you are uniquely able to contribute. Between the balance of limitation and engagement, we find humility.

Humble parents know this: God does not need you. He may choose to work through you, but he also might work in spite of you. This posture is the antidote for the feeling of not feeling qualified. Of course you are not qualified! There was never any qualification process to begin with.

The fact that God does not need you but invites you into the process of discipleship is not him keeping you at arm's length. Instead, it's God's loving protection for you. Your heart is not made to handle the weight of the burden of discipleship. Trusting God with our kids' discipleship keeps us from pride when things work out well and crushing despair when things don't.

From the unique place you occupy as your child's parent, there are two key responsibilities that are uniquely yours: Put them where God has promised to work, and prepare them for eternity.

1. Put your children in the places where God has already promised to work.

From the beginning, God has ordained a few things as essential to the life of his followers: the word of God, prayer, and the sacraments of the Lord's Supper and baptism. We call these the "ordinary means of grace" because God has promised to work through these ordinary things to bring salvation. Where are these things found? In the church.

You may have been hurt by the church. You may have hurt the church as well. Let this direct statement do nothing to minimize the pain you may carry with you: Your children need to be a part of a gospel-rich church. Your children need to sit under the preached word of God week in and week out simply because this is how God has planned to bring salvation to his people.

Let me go a step further. Your children need to go to a church that meets in-person. Virtual church was an emergency solution most churches transitioned to during COVID. However, that emergency solution became too many people's default.[11] Only adding to this problem is our desire to "make up for lost time." Having been deprived for the better part of two years, we have now crammed our family schedules full of sports, extracurriculars, and trips. We simply have no time left for church.

While much has changed in the last decade, this simple fact remains: You and your children need to be in a physical location, at least weekly, with other Christians. They need visible, tangible reminders of the goodness of God in the sacraments. They need the nearness of God found in prayer. They need to gather with other disciples from all walks of life. They need to hear the old man in the pew behind them singing "Amazing Grace" for the ten-thousandth time. They need to watch the teenager, ten years down the road, walking faithfully with God. If Jesus calls the church his bride, and if he gave the keys of the kingdom to the church, then the church is essential to your child's discipleship.

2. Prepare them for eternity.

Discipleship is not about preparing your children to live better lives in this world. Read that again. Much of evangelical Christianity has been poisoned by the prosperity gospel. We may not believe God will make us millionaires, but we're sure that Jesus ought to make our lives more enjoyable and easier.

However, Jesus tells his disciples in John 16 that he is training them not so they will live better, more productive, and less encumbered lives. Instead, he tells them about the glories of the gospel—"that in me you may have peace" (verse 33). Why? "In this world you will have trouble. But take heart! I have overcome the world" (verse 33 NIV).

---

11. For every family, there may be exceptional circumstances and seasons where virtual church is the best choice. However, every family should move back toward in-person worship as soon as it is feasible and wise. If a church or family's worship experience is only virtual, there cannot be an experience of all the ordinary means of grace or a real, physical community that supports one another.

Today, a disturbing amount of evangelical Christianity focuses on making Earth a more comfortable place. To that end, we put our hopes in political figures, education, morality, fiscal policies, and international relations. These areas just listed are worthy of our attention and care as humans made in God's image. We are to be caretakers and stewards of God's good creation (more on this in a later chapter).

But when anything (literally anything) is put forward as the *thing* that will finally bring us peace—be it a new house, president, school, friendship, or athletic pursuit—we miss what Jesus explicitly told his disciples: "In this world, you will have trouble." Discipling our children toward the kingdom of God means they will live at odds with the world. Faithful disciples will take the narrow path and make choices that will ostracize them. They will have trouble because Jesus promised they would, and Jesus tends to be a man of his word.

This work of preparing our children to face trouble is very, very good work. Paul says it this way: "For I consider that the sufferings of this present time are not worth comparing with the glory that is to be revealed to us" (Romans 8:18).

It isn't worth wasting a millisecond of Paul's time, energy, or mental space to even consider that his suffering in this life is not worth it. Remember, this is Paul, who was jailed, beaten, and shipwrecked and became the laughingstock of major first-century cities. From his conversion right to the very end was nothing but hardship, and yet Paul ties his hopes to eternity. Paul understands that while tomorrow may be different, it will simply bring different challenges.

In a world that tells them they have limitless potential, your children will eventually come face-to-face with their own shortcomings. In a world that tells them they can be anything they want to be and have everything they desire, your children will experience disappointment. It's for this reason that parents who lead their children to God with eternity in mind can literally change the world. That's not an overstatement. Any parent can change the world, and it starts with going home and preparing our children for trouble.

When children expect trouble in this life *and* place their hope in eternity, they become resilient people who can bear the burdens of life and live as faithful and fruitful witnesses of the grace of God. Can you imagine the adults they'll become? Perhaps they'll be able to stay married even in the face of immense hurt. Maybe they'll stay in a challenging but necessary job instead of finding something with the promise of greater ease or "flexibility" every few years. Likely, they will feel less of a need to detach with the assistance of substances, video games, and pornography. Instead, when life becomes challenging, they'll think, *Yeah, I expected this, and it's a good thing my well-being doesn't depend on this going well. The sufferings of this present time are not worth comparing with the glory that is to be revealed in me.*

What Will This Require?

Most research on human motivation shows that we must have a significant *why* to take sustained action toward a goal. In other words, we must feel a sense of purpose behind the things we do in order to consistently do the things we do. Goals without a motivating *why* become graveyards of good intentions. My son's bedroom comes to mind when I think of these graveyards. Despite his parents' repeated requests to keep his room at least moderately sanitary, he lacks a purposeful *why*. In fact, our demands of cleanliness may only serve to demotivate him.

While Sarah and I are only trying to teach our child some life-management skills, he likely hears something different, and it goes like this: When it comes to my room, I am *useful* inasmuch as I'm able to keep it clean.

The concept of usefulness is bizarre for most of us to consider as it's very nearly the air we breathe. Western culture subconsciously esteems usefulness.

We are raised to be useful, productive citizens. You may not know who you are outside of your usefulness. You likely strive to become more useful and look for others who are useful to you. And yet, usefulness is a terrible long-term motivator. God made us to transcend mere usefulness: we are most motivated when we know we are worthy of delight simply because of who we are.[12]

Usefulness is not useless, however. In fact, it is a good part of what God made us for. The problems come when we elevate usefulness above or even alongside our core identity of worthiness. Consider the creation account of Genesis 1:26. God proclaims his delight in man's identity ("Let us make man in our image, after our likeness") before he declares his usefulness ("let them have dominion").

Think of it this way: You are useful to the economy until your money dries up. You are useful to your job until they decide to replace you. You are useful to your children's happiness until they hate you. Your body is useful until it experiences more pain than pleasure. My son is useful so long as he keeps a clean room? Yikes!

What would be more motivating to my son is to remind him again and again that we value him for who he is wholly outside of the condition of his room. This is not some emotional platitude; it's simply our attempt to see our son how God sees him. We do not need him to keep his room clean. Instead, we want him to see his bedroom as a gift from God. It's a place he can rest from a hard day's work. It's a place he can create, build, dream, and grow. It is a place he's called to steward, but it is not a place where he earns or loses our affection. Only when he understands this will his care for his bedroom move beyond a means to prove his usefulness. Only then will he truly learn to steward what God has provided.

If a child's life is hard to imagine, consider your own adult-sized challenges.

---

12. Much of the content in the next few pages is greatly influenced by Alan Noble, *On Getting Out of Bed* (InterVarsity Press, 2023), 97–99.

I'd imagine you naturally gravitate toward friendships where you're loved simply for who you are, not for your skills, gifts, or abilities. As you drift into middle adulthood, for example, you'll find freedom if your marriage is not primarily predicated on physical attraction but is deeply rooted in the safety of being simultaneously known for all your flaws and yet endlessly loved.

If what I'm describing sounds a lot like how God sees you, you're right. God is vastly different from the world: It's not because you are *useful* to God that he is interested in you. He doesn't need anything from you.

Sadly, we've raised a generation of Christians who wrongly believe that God is waiting around for them to *do something*. Have we forgotten Paul's words before the Areopagus? "The God who made the world and everything in it, being Lord of heaven and earth, does not live in temples made by man, *nor is he served by human hands, as though he needed anything*, since he himself gives to all mankind life and breath and everything" (Acts 17:24-25, emphasis mine).

God did not make you and sustain you so that you can be useful to him. He created you and loves you because he wanted to and it brings him glory to do so. To God, your life is a good act of creation and it remains good despite your sin, age, skills, beauty, strength, and charisma. You are his delight without qualification.

When we see God in this way, he naturally becomes the reorienting *why* of our lives. If God loves you *that* deeply—and he does—why wouldn't you want to know him? Our hearts desperately long to hear that we matter simply because we exist, not because we have checked the boxes that make someone proud of us.

The only truly life-giving *why* for you and your family is a whole-hearted pursuit of God. From this posture, we see that our existence transcends that of usefulness. We are beloved. We are wonderfully made. We can work, rest, love, care, mourn, and find happiness without the worry that our usefulness to God is in jeopardy. We are safe. That type of rootedness is the place from which God disciples us.

A clean house can be a wonderful place for hospitality and a well-ordered life. However, it requires our utility and will leave us feeling empty if we cannot achieve a self-determined level of cleanliness.

Youth sports are fine tools that help us experience the goodness of creation and friendship, but they are terrible *whys* because they demand our performance.

Your career is perhaps the place where you will do the most good in the world. And yet, it asks that you remain sharp, intelligent, and…useful.

You were designed for only one ultimate *why*: God.

The apostle Paul knew of this *why* when he wrote to the Philippians that he counted all his accomplishments and pedigree a loss. Why? "Because of the surpassing worth of knowing Christ Jesus my Lord" (Philippians 3:8).

If Paul, who had perhaps the most intimate experience with Jesus of anyone on this side of heaven, found knowing Christ to be his *why*, then perhaps we could learn something from him. The surpassing worth of knowing God is the *why* that gives us the wherewithal to…

   …pursue being discipled by Jesus (your kids aren't the only ones who need him).

   …surround ourselves with community, even when it seems costly.

   …invest in a church that loves Jesus.

   …invite and trust others who love Jesus to take active roles in our children's discipleship.

As we experience the blessings of discipleship, what may feel stressful right now will turn into something we love, which is good news—because we build our lives on the things we love, almost subconsciously.

So, what is your *why* when it comes to raising your children? If it is to shape them into useful citizens of this world, your journey and theirs will be full of stress and exhaustion. They won't meet the mark, ever. As Jesus said, they *will* have trouble. Eventually, their usefulness won't be enough, will wear out, and will become irrelevant.

But if your *why* is to form your children into citizens of heaven who know that God delights in them with no qualifications, they will become humble, fruitful people who enjoy God and love their neighbors. Though they will struggle in this world, they will glory in the new heavens and new earth.

So far we have a good recipe for building your *why*, but it is missing one crucial ingredient.

Captivation, Not Agreement

Often, we mistake mental agreement for heartfelt captivation. Almost all Christian parents agree with the concept of discipleship. They see the value in it. They see the need for it. Perhaps those who have agreed with the idea will take it out for a spin—that is, until it gets hard. Difficulty will break anyone who merely agrees with a concept. But those who are captivated at an emotional level are like immovable trees planted by streams of water.[13]

God made us to be captivated by a story bigger than ourselves. You see this all over the Bible. Psalm 8:3-4 captures this when the writer sings, "When I look at your heavens, the work of your fingers, the moon and the stars, which you have set in place, what is man that you are mindful of him, and the son of man that you care for him?" Or look at Psalm 19:7-10:

> The law of the Lord is perfect, reviving the soul; the testimony of the Lord is sure, making wise the simple; the precepts of the Lord are right, rejoicing the heart; the commandment of the Lord is pure, enlightening the eyes; the fear of the Lord is clean, enduring forever; the rules of the Lord are true, and righteous altogether. More

---

13. Psalm 1.

to be desired are they than gold, even much fine gold; sweeter also than honey and drippings of the honeycomb.

I'm just going to say what's on my heart here. The words of Psalm 8 and Psalm 19 and the mood in the room of most American churches on Sunday morning could not be any different. It's like a big game of "one of these things is not like the other." Psalm 8 and 19 make me blush. They thrill my heart. They lift my eyes to the spectacular work of God, while many evangelical churches look like a snooze fest. People don't sing. They sit stoically, hands folded like they're at supper with the Queen of England. They scurry out the back door as soon as the whole fiasco is over.

Christians are bored, but it's not because God is boring. We've simply become distracted by lesser pleasures. Parents who agree that God is good but are bored by him will raise children who are also bored by God.

But here's the thing. Nobody who knows God through how he reveals Himself in the Bible and through the work of the Holy Spirit could possibly find him to be boring. No, instead what has happened is many have become content to set their affections on other things.

C.S. Lewis famously said,

> It would seem that Our Lord finds our desires not too strong, but too weak. We are half-hearted creatures, fooling about with drink and sex and ambition when infinite joy is offered us, like an ignorant child who wants to go on making mud pies in a slum because he cannot imagine what is meant by the offer of a holiday at the sea. We are far too easily pleased.[14]

In the following chapter, we'll try to set aside the mud pies and lift our eyes to recapture the joy offered to those who become disciples of Jesus.

---

14. C.S. Lewis, *The Weight of Glory* (HarperCollins, 2001), 26.

This requires parents who are willing to do three things.

1. Relinquish control of what only God can do.

A few years ago, I began my obsession with having a perfect lawn. I began by applying fertilizer one morning, but by the afternoon, there was no noticeable difference in its lushness (imagine that!). So I applied more. The next morning, there was still no change. So I applied a third and heavier dose of fertilizer. Over the next two weeks, my grass died. The fertilizer was not working on my (albeit ridiculous) timeline, so I seized control of the situation (while also not reading the instructions). The result was the opposite of the intended effect. If I had been patient, my lawn would have been beautiful in three to five days.

I see a lot of parents who seize control when they don't see the results of discipleship in the time frame they expect. Others completely give up. But a fight-or-flight response to discipleship is an anxious grab for control of the uncontrollable. Proverbs 21:1 reminds of this: "The king's heart is a stream of water in the hand of the LORD; he turns it wherever he will." And so it is with your child's heart. Your anxious toil does little good next to the work of God's effortless hand.

2. Accept responsibility for your part in discipleship.

While God is your child's primary discipler, you are very likely the primary person he invites into that process. You are the one who introduces your children to God. You are the one who models what a relationship with God looks like. You are the one who engages them in conversation about what God is doing in their lives. Paul writes in Romans 10:14, "How are they to believe in him of whom they have never heard?" Our job is to put our children in the places where they can hear the good news.

3. Become captivated by the work of God.

Let it be the *why* that reorients your family's life. Every member of your family has a God-given desire to pursue beauty, excellence, goodness, and a host of other qualities that are only fully found in God's presence. Have you allowed your God-given desire to be partially fulfilled in lesser pleasures rather than allowing them to propel you to a fullhearted experience of God?

Much of the rest of this book will dance between the paradigm of parental responsibility and God's gracious and active role in discipleship. But first, to dance this dance day after day—not only well but willingly—requires us to step backward and recapture a sense of what Jesus knew of discipleship.

CHAPTER 2

Covered in Dust

One of our children is especially adventurous. I can always tell where he's been, what he's eaten, or what he's done by the mud, marker, grease, or chocolate smeared somewhere on his face or clothing. Disciples in Jesus's time were not too dissimilar, and this bears significance as we think of discipleship for children today.

Making disciples in the first century was never simply about knowledge. Instead, it was about the millions of everyday decisions we make in light of our knowledge and our experiences of the goodness of God. It was about the subtle choices and convictions that shape us into people with a sense of right and wrong, good and evil. The work of God changes us into people who find beauty in what God finds beautiful; what God finds delightful also delights us.

Discipleship was laced into every part of life. It would have never occurred to a first-century Jew to relegate discipleship to one day a week or even ten minutes each day. Just do a simple internet search for

"Jewish calendar." Notice there are between three and eighteen days *per month* that require observance, fasting, celebration, or reenactment. Being a disciple in the first century controlled every aspect of your life, including family, friends, and careers. Consider this scene, one of the first in Jesus's ministry.

"While walking by the Sea of Galilee, Jesus saw two brothers, Simon (who is called Peter) and Andrew his brother, casting a net into the sea, for they were fishermen. And he said to them, 'Follow me, and I will make you fishers of men.'" No introductions. No "Hey! How are the fish biting today?" niceties. Then something happens that today would be inconceivable: "Immediately they left their nets and followed him." Something about Jesus prompted these men to trust him and leave their only source of income behind: "Going on from there [Jesus] saw two other brothers, James the son of Zebedee and John his brother, in the boat with Zebedee their father, mending their nets, and he called them. Immediately they left the boat and their father and followed him" (Matthew 4:18-22).

You've likely read this story and thought, *Great…Jesus is gathering his disciples*. But there is so much more to the story. Ink was expensive in the first century, so small details make a big difference.

This scene in Matthew 4 only makes sense in the context of a first-century understanding of discipleship—the type Jesus would have been raised in. You see, Jesus grew up in the region of Galilee. The people of this region were in possession of the first five books of the Bible, known as the Torah. *Torah*, translated into English, simply means *instruction*. The Torah was the center of life for the Jewish people and the focal point of their education system.

Most Jewish children, beginning at the age of six, went to school to start learning the Torah. These schools were held in the local synagogue with a rabbi as the teacher. The first level of education lasted until a child was around the age of ten. At this level, most children would memorize the Torah word for word. That's right! Genesis, Exodus, Leviticus, Numbers, and Deuteronomy—all memorized by the time today's children enter fourth grade. That's one book per year for those keeping score at home. It's a massive accomplishment that requires an exceptional level of dedication.

By the end of this stage, most children no longer went to school. Instead, they were sent home to learn the family business or trade—farming, carpentry, sewing, weaving, or something else beneficial to the community at large. But the best students entered the next phase of school. Over the next four years, children memorized the entirety of the Hebrew Scriptures. So by the time these students were fourteen, they had memorized Genesis through Malachi. Thirty-nine books committed to memory over a nine-year period. To achieve such a feat today would require a radical reorientation of your life.

At this point, the majority of these students joined the first wave of students who had been sent home at the age of ten to learn the family trade. But if you were at the top of your class, at the age of fourteen, you could identify a rabbi you admired and wanted to learn from. This very small percentage of high-achieving teenagers (think of them as the ones with perfect college entrance exam scores) applied to the rabbi of their choosing to become one of his disciples. In the first century, when you applied to be a rabbi's disciple, you were essentially saying, "I don't just want to know the things you know. *I want to be like you.*"

Now, each rabbi had a different set of practices and principles for what it meant to follow God. These requirements were known as a rabbi's yoke. And so the way you spoke of this was by saying you wanted to "take on a rabbi's yoke." Hold on to that because it will become important in a moment.

After you applied to a rabbi, they examined you to see not only how much of the Scriptures you knew but what your understanding of them was. Each rabbi wanted to answer the question, Does this child have what it takes to follow me? Can they take on my yoke? Do they love God with all their heart, mind, soul, and strength? This examination wasn't necessarily concerned with how much knowledge you possessed. By this point in the process, everyone was remarkably intelligent. Instead, the rabbi looked for marks of integrity, resiliency, awareness—today, we might call this *emotional intelligence*.

Once the examinations were complete, a very small number of applicants were accepted to follow the rabbis, while the rest—you guessed it—were sent home to learn the family trade. Even the cream of the crop, the ones with perfect scores, were sent home. But if you were the best of the best of the best, you were selected to be a disciple, and the rabbi would say, "Come, follow me."

Once selected, you left everything you knew and devoted your entire life to becoming like your rabbi. For the next fifteen years, a rabbi's disciple followed him from town to town and synagogue to synagogue, learning, watching, asking, listening. Disciples literally lived in the shadows of their rabbis. They wanted to know everything about them—how they interacted with others, what habits they cultivated, when they rested, and when they worked.

Paved roads and manicured lawns were not a thing back then, so the streets were filled with dirt, mud, and dust. There were no cars, buses, or trains, so if you wanted to get anywhere, you had to walk. No need for "getting in your steps" in first-century Judea and Galilee. That was a given.

Because of the amount of walking closely behind their rabbi through dusty streets and sitting at the feet of their rabbi on dirt floors, faithful disciples were said to be "covered in the dust of their rabbi."[1] People knew who they were and where they had been because their bodies were caked in dust, much like how

---

1. The source of this saying is the Mishnah, Avot 1:4. (The Mishnah is a collection of rabbinic thought from 200 BC to AD 200 that still forms the core of Jewish belief today.) The quotation is from Yose ben Yoezer. (yo-EHZ-er). He was one of the earliest members of the rabbinic movement and lived about two centuries before Jesus:

> Let thy house be a meeting-house for the wise;
> and powder thyself in the dust of their feet;
> and drink their words with thirstiness.
> [Pirqe Aboth 1:4, Charles Taylor, trans. (United Kingdom: University Press, 1877)].

my son's mouth is often covered in powdered doughnut residue (while he pleads his innocence!).

Most rabbis began teaching around the age of thirty, which is precisely the age that Jesus began his ministry. The beginning of Matthew's Gospel records these first moments, and it is there that Jesus walks along the shore, calling to a group of fishermen, "Come, follow me" (Matthew 4:19 NIV).

This has enormous implications for discipleship both then and today. With three words, Jesus completely shifted the paradigm of discipleship and created an enduring legacy right up to the present day. Here's what I mean: If these men were fishermen by trade, that means they were not smart enough or able enough to merit the tutelage of a rabbi.

This means they were not the best of the best.

They were sent home.

They learned the family business.

They were phenomenally average people.

They didn't even have the chance to apply to be disciples.

This rabbi, though, was different. Jesus looked at these men who didn't make the cut and effectively said, "I think you can do this. I believe you can follow me. Out of everyone I could select, I want you."

What did Jesus see in these men? We get some hints just one chapter later…

> Blessed are the poor in spirit, for theirs is the kingdom of heaven.
> Blessed are those who mourn, for they shall be comforted.
> Blessed are the meek, for they shall inherit the earth.
> Blessed are those who hunger and thirst for righteousness, for they shall be satisfied.
> Blessed are the merciful, for they shall receive mercy.
> Blessed are the pure in heart, for they shall see God.
> Blessed are the peacemakers, for they shall be called sons of God.
> Blessed are those who are persecuted for righteousness' sake, for

theirs is the kingdom of heaven.
Blessed are you when others revile you and persecute you and utter
all kinds of evil against you falsely on my account.
Rejoice and be glad, for your reward is great in heaven, for so they
persecuted the prophets who were before you (Matthew 5:3-12).

Disciples of Jesus are not necessarily intelligent. They don't have to prove themselves. They don't have to submit a résumé or pass examinations. The disciples Jesus looks for know that all Jesus requires to follow him is…nothing. That is the big, bold, unflinching, not-so-hidden message of Jesus's selection of fishermen as his disciples.

What about Jesus's words about his yoke later in the Gospel of Matthew? Remember, a yoke was the set of practices and principles rabbis passed on to their disciples: "Come to me, all who labor and are heavy laden, and I will give you rest. Take my yoke upon you, and learn from me, for I am gentle and lowly in heart, and you will find rest for your souls. For my yoke is easy, and my burden is light" (Matthew 11:28-30).

At this point in Jesus's ministry, the Jewish people were under immense pressure from the Pharisees and scribes to follow lengthy lists of requirements to earn God's favor. If you couldn't live up to the standard, you were a failure—like one of those sent home to learn the family trade. Yet here Jesus says, "Come to me…I will give you rest…I am gentle and lowly in heart…my yoke is easy, and my burden is light."

The measure of being Jesus's disciple is not how much you know or do. The measure—get this—is how well you can rest. The active decision to rest is a posture of complete trust. It is an admission that the best thing for me right now is to simply be. Nothing to do. Nothing to achieve. No lists to make my way through. You can rest.

It's clear from the first day of his ministry that Jesus was different. His following went on to include men and women, the educated and uneducated, the rich and the poor, the weak and the strong, the best of the best and the worst of the worst. These ragtag disciples, co-laborers, and followers were covered in the dust of their rabbi.

What did these first disciples learn? What can we learn today from this picture of Jesus as our discipler?

You're a Saint, Not a Sinner

Jesus believes you can be like him. He even tells his disciples at one point,

> No longer do I call you servants, for the servant does not know what his master is doing; but I have called you friends, for all that I have heard from my Father I have made known to you. You did not choose me, but I chose you and appointed you that you should go and bear fruit and that your fruit should abide, so that whatever you ask the Father in my name, he may give it to you (John 15:15-16).

Jesus calls his disciples because he knows they have what it takes to follow him—not because they are superior students but because of what God will do through them as a result of the power of his Spirit at work in them.[2]

Our children need to hear that Jesus believes in them, that he is cheering them on. Too many churches and leaders beat the drum of telling everyone how awful they are. Every week it's more of "You're a sinner, you're a sinner, you're a sinner." Proponents of this philosophy of ministry insist that we will never know how much we need Jesus if we don't know how much we need to be saved. I agree, but it must be balanced with the message of sainthood if we are to honor the way God actually speaks of us in the Bible.[3]

---

2. Ephesians 3:14–21.
3. Matthew 27:52; Romans 1:7; 8:27; 1 Corinthians 1:2; 6:1–2; 2 Corinthians 13:13; Ephesians 1:1; 2:19; 4:12, just to name a few places believers are referred to as *saints* in the New Testament.

We also need to ask the question, If the Holy Spirit prompts faith in our children by convicting them of their sin, will they find following Jesus to be good news?[4] Or will they find a mere caricature of Jesus, another accuser?

Now, please do not hear what I'm not saying. It is true that we sin and can only hope in the saving grace of Jesus.[5] However, this is only one part of who we are. Those who belong to God have been called saints.

So, what does *saint* mean? In its most basic sense, a saint is a "holy one," someone who is set apart for God's special purposes.[6] As a result, every follower of Jesus is a saint. In most of his letters, the apostle Paul refers to the recipients as saints, including the church at Corinth, where there were significant moral and theological problems![7]

The New Testament writers draw their use of the word *saints* (holy ones) from the Old Testament. Particularly important is Exodus 19:6, where God refers to Israel as "a kingdom of priests and a holy nation." First Peter 2:9 applies this same language to believers: "You are a chosen race, a royal priesthood, a holy nation, a people for his own possession, that you may proclaim the excellencies of him who called you out of darkness into his marvelous light." What a profound honor it is to be a disciple!

Overwhelmingly, the Bible does not call Christians sinners. For instance, if we only look at the writings of Paul, he calls Christians saints forty times, but he virtually never calls Christians sinners. Even when he does, it is usually in reference to unbelieving Gentiles or in the past tense.[8] Rankin Wilbourne notes, "The biblical writers, addressing groups of people with debilitating and persistent sin, call their readers 'saints' (Eph. 1:1), even though the contents of these

---

4. John 16:7–11.
5. Romans 3:23–26.
6. Psalm 89:5.
7. 1 Corinthians 1:2, for example.
8. Galatians 2:15; Romans 5:8.

letters make clear their lives are far from saintly. It's an undeserved but enno-bling compliment! Saint! Become what you are."[9]

Why is this important? Social psychologists tell us that our bodies are wired to respond most durably to positive reinforcement. Positive reinforcement is the act of rewarding a behavior in order to encourage it to happen again in the future. For instance, if a child receives a compliment on their outfit, they are more likely to wear that outfit again. The best way to create long-lasting, endur-ing change is to reward behaviors you want to repeat. In God's wisdom, call-ing someone a saint is a positive reinforcement. How kind of God to create our bodies in this way and then use that very reinforcement response to form us into faithful believers!

Sinner, however, is received as a positive punishment (which is different than a negative reinforcement). Positive punishment is the act of adding a con-sequence to unwanted behavior to make it less appealing. An example of pos-itive punishment is adding more chores to the list when your child neglects their responsibilities. Our bodies are designed to respond most powerfully to positive punishment. It signals danger and produces immediate and noticeable short-term results. Leaders, parents, and teachers are drawn to the use of pos-itive punishment because they can literally see the response before their very eyes. However, positive punishment almost always fails to create productive, long-term change. In the long run, it leaves behind a wake of anxiety, fear, and paranoia. We do not develop feelings of trust and safety with those we associ-ate with positive punishment.

When we use the word *sinners* to address believing children who are disci-ples of Jesus, we may be well-intentioned and simply repeating what we've been told. However, using this terminology inaccurately is like giving our children microdoses of positive punishment. This is not only confusing to children; it's

---

9. Rankin Wilbourne, *Union with Christ* (David C. Cook, 2016), 184.

simply out of accord with how the Bible reads. Instead, our believing children need to know that they are *saints who sin*. Their primary identity is *saint*. Their alien compulsion is *sin*.[10]

You Succeed When You Rest

Jesus's yoke is easy, and his burden is light, but that does not mean we have an excuse for laziness. That is far from what Jesus means by "finding rest for your souls." Instead, what Jesus has in mind is an eternal rest, a sturdiness of the soul. In fact, Jesus picks up on a theme from Jeremiah. There, the prophet says, "Thus says the LORD: 'Stand by the roads, and look, and ask for the ancient paths, where the good way is; and walk in it, and find rest for your souls'" (Jeremiah 6:16). Finding rest for our souls is a search for the "good way," and when we find it, we "walk in it." This sounds a lot like the disciples who, upon being accepted by their rabbis, walk behind them, becoming covered in their dust.

I've always found the idea of owning pets strange. I know I'm in the minority, but there is just something unnatural about inviting an animal inside your home to live with you. And besides that, I currently have four other small living creatures who need me to feed and bathe them. I don't need one more.

Growing up, we had a dog named Betsy. I can vividly remember the day Betsy ran away from home. My parents ominously noted, "If we can't find her in the next day or two, she probably won't make it out there." (We found her, and Betsy went on to live a long, healthy life within the confines of our home.)

My parents' statement has always stuck with me. Why wouldn't Betsy have survived in the wild woods of suburban Melbourne, Florida? It was because she had learned to rest within our home.

Unlike wild dogs, who must constantly be on alert for danger, Betsy slept

---

10. Romans 7:15–25.

when she wanted, played when she pleased, and stared at the squirrels out the window for hours each day.

Unlike wild dogs, who scavenge for food and compete for scarce resources, Betsy relied on her two scoops of dog food provided for her at the same time every day.

Unlike wild dogs, who need to create and defend a territory, Betsy was well protected twenty-four hours a day.

Disciples who find rest for their souls are much like Betsy. We have come inside from the world and its unrelenting demands to be useful, flawless, and "somebody." Unlike Betsy, stepping away from the world has not made us weaker and more vulnerable. Instead, it has strengthened us as we rest in the strong arms of God.[11] We cast our cares on him.[12] We are never alone, but instead know his nearness when we are brokenhearted.[13] We can lay down our anxious striving, knowing that if he cares for the sparrow, he also cares for us. He clothes the flowers in royal splendor; will he not also clothe us?[14] Disciples of Jesus, covered in the dust of their rabbi, can rest secure knowing the harsh demands of the world have no hold on them.

We become like the sheep in Psalm 23:2 who "lie down in green pastures." These same sheep, who have been trained to rest under the reassuring, steady gaze of their shepherd, would never survive on their own. Disciples of Jesus are no different. Without the yoke of our rabbi, we would face the world alone. We would drown in anxiety. We'd either have to invent some false narrative about life to survive, or we would succumb to the pressure.

Our children need to know from the earliest age that being a disciple of Jesus is measured not in Bible verses memorized but in their willingness to rest—to

---

11. Isaiah 41:10.
12. 1 Peter 5:7.
13. Psalm 34:18.
14. Matthew 6:25–33.

trust that the same God who hung the stars in the sky is the one who knows every hair on their heads. They can relinquish control of their lives, find the good way, walk in it, and be covered in the dust of their rabbi.

Your Pedigree Means Nothing

If you've ever lived in a small town, you know that last names matter. It tells people who your parents are, where you stand in the social pecking order, and something of your potential in life. I've known young women from these communities who would not marry certain men because of the social stigma her new name would carry.

Every community has markers of social success. It's how we get by in life. We love to walk into a room, look around, and feel superior to at least one other person. It's why we love crime documentaries. We might be bad, but we aren't *that* kind of bad.

But in the kingdom of God, all social markers of success are declared null and void. Jesus intentionally selected uneducated, poor men to become his disciples. Along the way, he brought women into his leadership circle. He dined with sinners.[15] He healed the sick.[16] He cared for the prostitutes.[17] All people, from all walks of life, share one common story: We are made in God's image, suffer the consequences of sin, and cannot save ourselves. Even so, the tidal wave of social norms seeks to divide us into readily identifiable, stratified categories.

Pecking orders don't take long to crystallize for children, and it's happening earlier and earlier. My first grader can already tell you where she ranks in her class in terms of beauty, popularity, and intelligence. She needs to hear that

---

15. Matthew 9:10–17.
16. Matthew 8:14–15.
17. John 8:1–11.

none of those have any bearing on how Jesus feels about her. She needs to know, deep in her soul, that she is a part of a long line of people from every walk of life who Jesus gives one name to—children. He simply asks her, "Come, follow me."

Just look at what Paul says in Romans 10:

> For with the heart one believes and is justified, and with the mouth one confesses and is saved (verse 10).

No application. No résumé. Believe in your heart. Confess with your mouth.

> For the Scripture says, "Everyone who believes in him will not be put to shame" (verse 11).

No disciple of Jesus will experience the shame of rejection, only the welcome of their Savior.

> For there is no distinction between Jew and Greek; for the same Lord is Lord of all, bestowing his riches on all who call on him (verse 12).

No pedigree, talent, socioeconomic status, or IQ score earns you any favor. All are welcome simply because Jesus loves to give his riches to his children.

> For "everyone who calls on the name of the Lord will be saved" (verse 13).

One requirement…call on his name. That's it.

Paul later reminds the Ephesians that the "Gentiles are fellow heirs, members of the same body" (Ephesians 3:6). The *Gentiles?* To a first-century Jew, that was unconscionable. The Gentiles were savages, ruthless in belief and behavior. And yet here they are with a place equal to the Jews. Paul goes on to say in this passage that he, a Jew, is "the very least of all the saints" (Ephesians 3:8). While this is perhaps an overstatement, largely based on Paul's history of mistreating believers (to put it lightly),[18] it indicates how God's kingdom has decimated the traditional pecking order.

Our children desperately need to hear this. In the age of AI-generated photos and elementary-aged kids connected to any social media platform they want, children desperately need to hear that the gospel levels the playing field. It is the only thing that brings true humility—the ability to see people the way God sees them. What if we raised children who walked into a room merely to serve, listen, and empathize with the people there instead of sizing everyone up to figure out where they fit in? That would change the world. That sounds like living as disciples of Jesus, covered in the dust of their rabbi.

Discipleship Changes Everything

John the Baptist writes of Jesus, "The Father loves the Son and has given all things into his hand" (John 3:35). If Jesus is our teacher and our discipler, then he is unlike any rabbi the world has ever known. First-century rabbis had knowledge and practices to pass along, but what Jesus gives us is far, far greater—*all things*. Jesus echoes this at the end of his earthly ministry, saying, "All authority in heaven and on earth has been given to me" (Matthew 28:18). Paul writes later, in Romans, that "we are children of God, and if children, then heirs—heirs of God and fellow heirs with Christ, provided we suffer with him in order that we may also be glorified with him" (Romans 8:16-17).

All things, all authority, the very glory of God belong to God's children—disciples of Jesus.

Paul later states in his first letter to the Corinthians, "So whether you eat or drink or whatever you do, do it all for the glory of God" (1 Corinthians 10:31 NIV). All things, under the banner of the glory of God.

What we eat? For the glory of God.

---

18. Acts 7:58.

How we care for our bodies? For the glory of God.

What we learn at school? For the glory of God.

How we care for our teammates? For the glory of God.

In many ways, this echoes what Moses said centuries before: "Behold, to the LORD your God belong heaven and the heaven of heavens, the earth with all that is in it" (Deuteronomy 10:14).

One of the greatest mistakes of modern children's discipleship is that we've narrowly focused on knowledge—memory verses, catechisms, and so on. Don't hear what I'm not saying—knowledge is important. But knowledge is only a part of discipleship. Our children are whole people, not heads on sticks.

If we are to recapture some of what Jesus intended for discipleship, we'll need our children to be covered in the dust of their rabbi. Every nook and cranny. When we go on beach vacations, we find sand everywhere, in all our stuff, for *months* afterward—places we didn't even know sand could possibly get. Abraham Kuyper once said, "There is not a square inch in the whole domain of our human existence over which Christ, who is Sovereign over all, does not cry, Mine!"[19]

Discovering a more biblical and true vision for children's discipleship allows the dust of their rabbi to cover children, to find its way into the hidden places, the details of their lives. Discipleship like this requires us to view children as whole people—those with physical bodies, emotions, desires, needs, and yes—knowledge. Throughout this book, we'll explore many aspects of childhood discipleship that help build resilient disciples of Jesus, but first we need to see that discipling our children begins with us.

---

19. Michael R. Wagenman, *Engaging the World with Abraham Kuyper* (Lexham Press, 2019), 46.

CHAPTER 3

You're a Disciple Too

On Saturday mornings, give me a bag of orange slices, a bunch of sweaty boys, and a soccer field, and I am in heaven. I don't even mind that half the field ends up inside my car after muddy games. I grew up playing soccer. For stretches of time, I spent every weekend at the fields and a surprising number of weeknights at practice. Palm Bay Regional Park was my second home, and I loved every moment of it. Friendships forged, heartbreaking losses, upset wins, and yes…lots of orange slices.

My soccer-playing days are now well in the rearview mirror, but today I get the joy of coaching my boys' soccer teams. It is a blast. I actually feel a slight wave of depression when soccer season comes to a close.

Now, I don't mean to brag or anything…but parents request for their kids to be on my team. I think I know why. Out of the coaches in our league, a small number are as passionate about soccer as I am. The rest are very willing parents. We love them and their willingness, but kids' experiences on their teams are vastly different from the experience kids have on my team (to be fair, my team has lost to a few of the "very willing parent" teams).

The difference comes in this: My kids know from day one that I am serious about their enjoyment of soccer. They know that I love them, that I love soccer, and that I think they can love soccer together while building lifelong friendships. They hear my stories, feel my passion, and learn the intricacies of the game. In a way, they see someone who is covered in the dust of soccer. When they experience being around me and hear me believe in their potential, they want to be great. Some might say the way I coach soccer is a model for discipleship. Here are a few thoughts.

1. You can't microwave passion.

It is built by simply being around something you love for extended periods of time. I've spent thirty-five years in and around the game of soccer. The "very willing parent" coaches try hard, but their passion is lacking. Likewise, parents who spend consistent time with Jesus become grace-filled disciple-makers. Those who've been in the presence of Jesus are attractive to be around. We want to become like them.

2. Develop muscle memory.

Over the years, soccer has become reflexive. It's baked into my muscle memory. Those who have watched me play basketball say I defend on the basketball court like a soccer player. I can't help it; it's where my body naturally wants to go. In a similar way, parents growing in relationship with Jesus watch the Spirit work through them to cultivate reflexes of kindness, joy, goodness, and self-control. They look like the image of God everywhere they go. They become like what Paul describes: "For we are the aroma of Christ to God among those who are being saved and among those who are perishing" (2 Corinthians 2:15).

3. Be an empathetic presence.

Like any athlete, I've experienced the ups and downs of the sport I love. I've scored game-winning goals and had season-ending injuries. I've been the best on the team and rode the bench. I've been on great teams and some pretty awful ones. I know how to empathize with the highs and lows that come with playing soccer. Likewise, parents who experience the goodness of God know the tragedy and beauty of our attempts to live faithful lives. When children need a shoulder to cry on or a fellow believer to celebrate with them, they'll find that in parents who've needed the same.

Some of you may read these words and feel encouraged. You love the Lord and have faithfully led your children to him. You're energized to be a part of what God is doing in your life and the lives of your children.

Others of you may feel ambivalent about following Jesus. It's nice for some people, but you feel no compelling reason to invest any more than you already do in your relationship with Jesus. You don't necessarily mind being a Christian, but it just doesn't rise to the top of your priority list.

Still more of you may be in the boat most Christian parents find themselves in. You feel guilty that you're not more invested in following Jesus. You want your kids to love Jesus, but you'd be embarrassed if they knew how little time you spend reading the Bible or in prayer. You may also feel bad for holding expectations for them that you don't personally hold for yourself.

For all three of you, there is hope for something more:

> And we all, with unveiled face, beholding the glory of the Lord, are being transformed into the same image from one degree of glory to another. For this comes from the Lord who is the Spirit (2 Corinthians 3:18).

All of us, from the committed to the ambivalent to the guilty, are being transformed into the image of God from one degree of glory to another. There is always a starting point. There is always a next step for each of us. We all have one thing in common: We have room to grow.

How does someone grow as a Christian, especially as an adult with limited time? For some of you, just making it to this point in a book with the demands of work, school, and bedtimes is a feat in and of itself. Parents, hear this: You are in the most physically taxing season of your life. In ten or fifteen years' time, you won't be changing diapers, playing taxi driver, and taking up semipermanent residence at the ball fields. There will be different temptations in that season of life, but for now, the way you might cope with life is to give up on your needs to meet the needs of others (namely, the ones who write on your walls and feel the obnoxious need to wake you up from naps when Alexa won't play the right song during rest time).

While this coping may work in the short term, it will fail you and your family in the end. When we deny our God-given need for God, our hearts harden, wilt, and shrivel. What was once looked at as self-denial in the name of loving our children is now self-pity and exhaustion.

You need the words of Jesus: "Abide in me, and I in you. As the branch cannot bear fruit by itself, unless it abides in the vine, neither can you, unless you abide in me. I am the vine; you are the branches. Whoever abides in me and I in him, he it is that bears much fruit, for apart from me you can do nothing" (John 15:4-5).

Mom and Dad, the care you need is more than just a nap or a weekend away. You need to learn to abide in Christ. You can give yourself to your kids all day long while denying your spiritual needs, but you will wither and your fruit will rot.

Abiding in Prayer

Lots of people read the Bible. Not all of them have a relationship with Jesus. Prayer is where the Christian uniquely meets with the God of the universe. It is where God stoops low to listen to his people. In prayer, we sense God's delight in us.

Prayer is one of the disciplines God commanded his people to pursue (1 Thessalonians 5:17). God gives routines for his people that bring life. Prayer should always be one of the primary activities of Christians, whether we are raising disciples or not. However, I'd take note that it fills a special role for parents in at least two ways: (1) Prayer lifts us from the echo chamber of our own mind. When we become the only voice we listen to, anxiety grows, pride increases, and loneliness sets in. Parenting within the myopic confines of your own head is a recipe for disaster. (2) Parenting can be full of resentment. We resent our children. We resent their teachers. We resent the social media influencer who taught them words and phrases we wish they could unhear. Resentment hardens our hearts, and there are few resources parents need more than a soft heart. It is hard to resent those we pray for, so pray for your children, their teachers, and yes, the social media influencer.

Make it a daily habit to spend dedicated time in prayer. Pray with others. Pray in the car. Pray while you walk. Pray over the phone with friends. Write your prayers. Speak them out loud. If you miss a day, that's okay. Every day is new and a chance to begin again. My guess is that once you find a rhythm of prayer, you will crave it. Sitting at the feet of Jesus and speaking with him daily will change your life. How could it not?

If you're not sure where to begin, I would humbly suggest that you read a newer book on prayer (*A Praying Life* by Paul Miller is phenomenal) and pick up an older classic prayer book (*The Valley of Vision* compiled by Arthur Bennett will get you started). Doing so will help you have a contemporary cheering you on and a father showing you the way.

You may also try reading a psalm each day. Read it twice. Once out loud and once slowly to yourself. Pick a word, a line, a stanza that sticks out to you, and talk to God about it in prayer. You have no need to be formal. Speaking to God is a conversation. Talk to him like you would speak with a good friend. After all, he did call you a friend, right?[1]

Abiding in God's Word

There is no substitute for the Bible in your life. Not even a good devotional can replace it. God has revealed himself in one way and one way only: through his word. There are no shortcuts, cheat codes, or CliffsNotes that will suffice.

As I've worked with families over the years, I've found that people's biggest obstacle to daily Bible reading is that they haven't started. Starting is the hardest part. Anyone who's trained for a race knows this to be true. The first day is the most difficult. The first week will hurt. But once you start linking together consecutive weeks, your body begins to crave the exercise.

The same tends to be true with Bible reading. The best way to start is to begin. Do not wait for the perfect reading plan to come along. Do it now. Do it while it's hard. If you wait for a time when your kids are less demanding, you'll never make time for it. You'll just fill your time with other things. Trust me. If you're not a reader, begin by listening to a good audio Bible. You'll also find many great resources and podcasts to supplement your Bible listening.

The writer of Hebrews says of God's word, "The word of God is living and active, sharper than any two-edged sword, piercing to the division of soul and of spirit, of joints and of marrow, and discerning the thoughts and intentions of the heart" (4:12). Nothing else can do those things. If you commit yourself to prayer and to reading the Bible every day, you will be a changed person in a year. There is no way around it.

---

1. John 15:15.

Abiding in The Church

If you are not a part of a Bible-believing, grace-centered, gospel-oriented church, you need to be. It can be a big church or a small church. It may meet in a fancy building or a living room. You can wear a suit or a T-shirt. What matters is that you submit yourself to the ordinary means of God's grace, which are found in his church. Here are a few questions to consider as you look for a church.

1. **Is the teaching of the gospel central?** Church is not a place for personal soapboxes, political rallies, and platform building. Choose a church for your family where the gospel of grace is preached carefully, helpfully, and humbly.

2. **Is prayer central?** Does the church include prayer as a part of their worship service? Is the prayer also confessional in nature, going beyond asking for God's blessing? Do the leaders invite the congregation to participate in and lead in prayer, or is it centralized to just the staff team?

3. **Are the sacraments practiced?** Baptism and the Lord's Supper are two means of grace God uses to establish and mature his people. Do not join a church where these sacraments are not celebrated. They are commanded by Jesus, and we practice them in submission to him because we believe that through them, God works to strengthen his church.

4. **Do your children like going there?** Early in my parenting and ministry, I used to counsel parents, "Don't choose a church based on what your kids like." Today, I regret giving that counsel. Kids are members of your family. They are people with valuable opinions and feelings. Like it or not, their input is vital to your family system. If we wait until some imaginary day to include them

in family decisions, we may never include them (and will probably back the authoritarian truck over their souls a few times!).

5. **Is there a community you can join?** Do you meet people you can be friends with? Church is not a place to leave as soon as the benediction is over. It is a community of people growing together in Christ. Church will stick for your family if you can find camaraderie with others.

Getting to Know Yourself

When parents quickly abandon their needs to meet the needs of their children, our culture applauds. A certain amount of self-denial is good and right. It models the life of Christ, who laid down his life for us.[2]

But it also saddens me. This abandoning of needs can be a failure to set appropriate boundaries. We have learned to deny our own needs because other people's needs became more important, and we didn't develop the skill of saying "no." We learned to survive life instead of live it. We denied our hearts instead of honoring them.

Just a few days ago, I heard a high-ranking public official comment, "I've never cried. I'm not a weepy person. I'm not a sissy." How sad. This official is not strong; he is weak. He doesn't have the strength to admit he is fragile just like the rest of us.

In the long run, when we deny our hearts, we only harm ourselves and our children. We grow weary, and our children learn that they don't need boundaries either.

Parents who've lost touch with their hearts also have great difficulty living in the freedom of vulnerability the gospel invites us to. We become like turtles who

---

2. 1 John 3:16.

duck in our shells whenever we might be exposed as being what we actually are—human beings with liabilities and wounds. Parents, hear this: If you never share your failures, mistakes, hardships, and challenges with your children, you must realize that you're modeling something totally unattainable for them. You are literally living a duplicitous life in full view of those you love the most. Children of parents like this falsely learn that life ought to be free of failures, mistakes, hardships, and challenges. How could they not? So, when they inevitably encounter defeat, what do they do? The same thing as their parents: They hide. They lose touch with their hearts. And the cycle continues generation after generation.

Here's what we need to hear: The work of discipling our children comes in raising a child you can no longer see.

That child is you.

All the fears, joys, disappointments, and hopes of your five-, ten-, and fifteen-year-old selves are still *right there*. Until you attune with and care for the child in you, you will lack the fullhearted capacity to love and guide the children God has entrusted to you. Children rarely rise above their parents in maturity, be it socially, emotionally, or spiritually.

The origin of the phrase "You can't outrun your past" is lost to history by this point. It borders close enough to cliché that I'm embarrassed to use it. This week, I've conducted an unofficial, unsanctioned, imprecise experiment with the phrase.

To nearly every person around my age or older, I've asked the question, "You can't outrun your past. How does that sit with you?" I've asked co-workers, neighbors, and even the lady in the Starbucks drive-through.

The least emotional response was, "Yeah, that's really true." On the other end of the spectrum, I shared a few tears with friends as we wrestled anew with unmet expectations, longings, and the inevitable, even boring predictability of life.

Many believe they can walk out of their tragic childhoods and into the peaceful bliss of adulthood like one might close a Stephen King novel and open a volume of *Good Housekeeping*. It doesn't work that way…at all!

Without serious work, you will pass along the traumas of your childhood to your children. In the best of scenarios, unless you attune to God and to the child still living inside your body, you'll embody a do-good, try-harder morality while the gospel has yet to heal the wounds of your past.

We all need the serious application of the kindness, gentleness, hopefulness, and truthfulness of the gospel to our inner child. Doing so will allow us to heal and emotionally and spiritually show up for our children.

Do this with me for a moment. Find a comfortable place where you can be alone. Write the three most painful memories of your childhood on a sheet of paper. Close your eyes. Breathe deeply and slowly. Let your mind drift back to those memories. Allow the painful feelings to wash over you. Become curious about the child that still lives in your body. This won't be easy, but this is the work we all need to do.

What did you want, but you were denied?

Who did you need to be with, but you felt alone?

What words did you long to hear, yet you were met with silence?

What guidance did you need, but you had to figure it out instead?

Name the hopes you had that only ended in disappointment.

Talk to that child.

Tell them they deserved better.

Mourn with that child.

Grieve what they lost.

Be kind to them.

Speak to them like Jesus might…[3]

---

3. The following are stated as if from Jesus himself, based on these verses: Ephesians 3:18; Philippians 4:19; Zephaniah 3:17; Psalm 107:9.

May you have the power to understand…how wide, how long,
how high, and how deep my love is for you.
I will meet all your needs according to my riches.
You are my delight. I am glad you are here. I rejoice over you.
I will satisfy your longing soul and fill you with good things.

How did that feel? My guess is that if that was the first time you've done an exercise similar to this, it felt weird. That's okay. Do it every day for a week. Do it every week for a year.

As you gain compassion for what your childhood self needed but lacked, you'll gain compassion for yourself today. Then we can go and get the things we need to live faithfully with Jesus—prayer, the word of God, the church, exercise, friendships, a nap, a balanced breakfast, and hobbies. This work is not selfish. Only fullhearted parents possess the capacity to truly see their own children's hearts and meet them in the places they need us.

In his book *Safe House*, Joshua Straub says, "Both research and the Bible reveal that our capacity to love stems from experiencing, or knowing, we are loved. The Bible says that we love because God first loved us. You love because somebody else first loved you."[4]

As you give yourself to the practices identified in this chapter, may you feel that you are deeply delighted in and loved. May you see that Jesus longs not only for your children to be discipled but for you to become his disciple as well. Only then, when you know that you were loved by God before the mountains sprang from the earth, will you be able to love the children he has entrusted you with.

---

4. Joshua Straub, *Safe House* (Waterbrook Press, 2015), 17.

CHAPTER 4

Discipling with Delight

My first office was a rat's nest. Literally. It was an old converted garage, and few strides had been made to make it not look like an old converted garage. The indoor-outdoor carpet was a little more outdoor than it was indoor. The window AC would blow a puff of dust every time it kicked on, and it only had two settings: bone-chilling cold or fiery inferno. The first week, I thought the place smelled like mold, so I filled my new space with air fresheners and candles. A few years later, when I upgraded to a new office and moved, I discovered that my mold theory was not wrong. My other theories, developed over time, included mildew, asbestos, and the grave sites of formerly living rodents. All my theories proved correct in due time.

My first office reminded me of Milton in the movie *Office Space*. While our good friend Milton just wanted a stapler, I just wanted to survive being a children's director with as little lung scarring as possible. Too much to ask?

While that first office was an eye-opener in terms of unexpected working conditions, I did manage to write my first set of curriculum in that most uninspiring of places. It was a guide for children and families to help them become more outward facing in their relationships with non-Christians. I wanted them to simply acknowledge the existence of other human beings. To see the people around them the way God might. I longed for them to have curiosity about others so they might help their neighbors, friends, and the cashier at the grocery store imagine what it would be like to have a relationship with the God who hung each star in its place.

Understandably, most of what I wrote fifteen years ago has changed over time, but one part has remained the same. It's a scripted conversation I have with every child who comes through our ministry, so I've logged well over 1,000 of these by now—quite the sample size if you ask me! Here's how it goes…

I ask the child to tell me about a friend who likely does not go to church or have a relationship with Jesus. What are they like? Why are they friends? What do they enjoy doing together? Importantly, I allow the child to lead the conversation. I enter their world. I want them to feel that what they have to share about their friend has real value. In the end, I want to honor their friend because of the next question in the conversation.

"Let's say you and your friend are hanging out one day, and they ask you, 'Hey, I know that you and your family are Christians. You go to church and read the Bible and believe in Jesus. How would I become a Christian?'" I pause, "What would you tell them?"

Ninety-five percent of children respond with some variation of this: "I would tell them they are a sinner who needs to repent and receive the forgiveness God offers through his Son's death on the cross."

This is a good answer, but it is not a *great* answer for one simple reason: The gospel does not begin with sin. Instead, it begins with delight. If this shift feels foreign, and if the mental heresy alarm bells have already sounded, stay with me. How we begin when we talk about the gospel changes everything.

Many evangelicals believe the gospel begins in Genesis 3. You may know the story well: The serpent slithers up to Adam and Eve in all his gross sliminess and convinces them that God is not as good as they might think he is. After the first couple falls prey to the lies, sin enters the world, and God curses the serpent, saying one will come to crush his head. This is good news. But it is not *great* news because it ignores the two chapters before Genesis 3 and why Moses wrote Genesis in the first place.

Genesis, in its written form, was nowhere to be found when Israel wound up as slaves in Egypt. It wasn't around when Moses demanded of Pharaoh, "Let my people go!" This may be hard for us to imagine, but those first generations of Israelites had nothing but oral traditions and stories passed down from grandparents. Following God, in many ways, looked quite different from how it looks for us today.

Sometime after the Exodus, however, Moses wrote Genesis. He wrote for a specific reason. God's people, his treasured possession, had been slaves for around 400 years. That is a long time. Four hundred years ago, America was just beginning its own evil empire of slavery, and the Declaration of Independence was still 150 years away.

Four hundred years changes people, and Israel was no different. Their identity dramatically shifted from God's beloved children—heirs of the promises made to Abraham—to the lowest place on the Egyptian socioeconomic ladder. They became little more than ancient assembly line workers doing the same meaningless, dirty job day after day after day.

Not only had they changed socially, but they had also changed spiritually. In Egypt, there was no such thing as Yahweh—the one true God. Instead, Pharaoh (a mere man) was worshipped as a god. He was said to be in charge of thousands of gods—gods who controlled war, the sun, insects, and reptiles. One of my favorites is Amenet, a goddess who welcomed the dead to the afterlife with food and drink. A divine waitress of sorts, you might say!

This polytheistic understanding of Egypt helps make a lot of sense of the Exodus: Pharaoh, you think there are gods of the sun, bugs, diseases, reptiles, and death? Actually, there is one true God who controls them all, and you are utterly powerless against him.

This understanding also helps make sense of the aftermath of the Exodus. On the heels of 400 years in Egypt, Israel was now functionally, emotionally, and spiritually more Egyptian than Israelite. These are the same people who made golden calves to worship in Exodus 32. While this moment in Israel's history was a catastrophic show of unfaithfulness, it does help make sense of where this bizarre impulse may have originated.

Into this extraordinarily atypical cultural moment, Moses wrote the book of Genesis to unwind 400 years of lies, to tell the truth about who God is, and to renarrate the lives of former slaves. What would these Israelites have heard?

Our God made all things. There are no little gods who made the stars and the water and the animals. One God, our God, made it all.

Our God does not struggle. He creates by speaking. Nothing hinders him.

Our God made us very good. We are the pinnacle of his creation.

Our God is the center of the story, not us.

Our God delights in us. We are not slaves.

The gospel, the good news of God, begins with delight. This is not a creative reformulation of the gospel. It is simply how God chose to tell the story. Simply put, God's story of good news does not begin with us. Instead, it begins with him, with what he freely wants to do, not under compulsion or pressure from anyone or anything. It is clear as day to any reader that God wants to both delight in us and have us know that we are his delight.

God's creative power stretches the entire span of the Bible. Genesis 1:1 begins, "In the beginning, God created the heavens and the earth." God is the best storyteller because, in the final chapter, he has John write these words: "Then I saw a new heaven and a new earth" (Revelation 21:1).

Lesslie Newbigin comments on these bookends of the Bible: "The Bible is unique among the sacred books of the world's religions in that it is in structure a history of the cosmos. It claims to show us the shape, the structure, the origin, and the goal not merely of human history, but of cosmic history."[1]

The most central, boiled-down message of the Bible is the good news of God's creative, redemptive, and restorative work of the entire universe. He delights in every tree he ever made, but even more than that…he delights in you, his child. He does not hold us at arm's length until we prove our sincerity or morality. Instead, he sent his only Son to suffer the death we deserve so that we would get what Jesus deserves—eternal, never-ending delight in the presence of God. The sacrifice of his only Son preserves and protects his delight in us.

When Jesus was resurrected, he showed himself to be a second Adam, a new beginning.[2] We get to experience that newness now, in this life: "If anyone is in Christ, he is a new creation" (2 Corinthians 5:17). Becoming a Christian does not simply add one more good thing to our résumés. It doesn't merely clean us up and help us get our act together. Instead, it makes us new. God delights in doing this work in us. It is not a struggle. This work is, in fact, God's priority. It is the work of a Father who delights in his children.

This does not mean our lives are devoid of sin and suffering. Paul goes on in 2 Corinthians to say we are "sorrowful, yet always rejoicing" (6:10). Ray Ortlund sums it up with this helpful anecdote:

---

1. Lesslie Newbigin, *The Open Secret: An Introduction to the Theology of Mission* (Eerdmans, 1995), 30–31.
2. 1 Corinthians 15:45.

Each of us is like a homeless man who sleeps under a bridge and eats out of dumpsters. One day a limousine pulls up, and out steps an attorney, who hands him a letter. A long-lost uncle has died and left him a fortune. The check will arrive in a few days. Suddenly, the cardboard shelter doesn't feel so hopeless. He can live with it for a while longer. A vast fortune is coming.[3]

I appreciate this illustration on many levels. Here's why…

1. Our normal state on this side of heaven is to feel homeless. To feel at home in this world is to be complacent and to have settled for lesser pleasures than what God longs to give us. There is a sort of discomfort for the Christian, like a square peg trying to fit in a round hole. It's a struggle, it won't work, and that is a very good thing.

2. The homeless man did nothing to earn the fortune. It belonged to him simply on the basis of his uncle's kindness. Nothing in the homeless man's constitution was worthy of such a gift. We, too, receive the gift of God's kindness despite our sins and our best attempts at morality.

3. The fortune has been promised but does not yet fully belong to the homeless man. His day-to-day struggle has not been replaced with endless goodness…yet. But because he knows that a vast fortune is coming, he can bear the grim reality of the present. Likewise, Christians can bear the weight of untold suffering because we know an eternity of untold joys awaits us.

---

3. Ray Ortlund, *The Gospel* (Crossway, 2014), 54.

Beyond honoring God by telling his whole story, why is it critical to begin the gospel with delight, especially when it comes to our children?

First Impressions

A great number of social researchers have studied the science behind our first impressions of people. While these impressions are not always reliable, they tend to be quite sticky.

When we purchased our first home, it took us no time at all to decide which agent we trusted. Alice Maxwell was friendly, organized, and confident. We didn't need to see her résumé to form an impression. Her presence told us everything we needed to know. Thankfully, we were right!

Nearly every credible study shows that our first (and often lasting) impressions of others form in less than seven seconds, regardless of age. Our children, like adults, feel safe or unsafe with people, places, and things quickly. *Very quickly.*

God knows this. Of course he does. He made our minds work this way. So it should come as no surprise that the undeniable message of the first two chapters of the Bible is that he delights in us. When someone delights in us, we are drawn to them. We feel safe and invited.

Cognitive Development

I will discuss children's developing brains in a later chapter, but an initial mention is warranted here. Adults often take for granted the skill of holding two truths in tension, where seemingly contradictory statements can mutually exist without negating the truthfulness of the other. For example, I love and hate Christmas. I love the sense of spiritual renewal and the joy of spending time with family. However, Christmas is my busiest season as a pastor and small business owner. I often feel stretched thin and resent the demands on my schedule (and bank account…seriously…being a parent at Christmas is way more expensive than anyone tells you!).

Living as a Christian involves a similar scenario of two truths. We are simultaneously sinful, and yet the Bible repeatedly reminds us that, in Christ, we are saints. This sinner-saint paradigm is the tension of the Christian life, and it is an abstract concept. Typically, children do not have the developmental capacity to comprehend abstract concepts until the age of eleven to sixteen, and even then, it is slow to develop. Later in this book, we will learn about the preoperational and concrete stages of cognitive development. While children develop a great deal from birth through age eleven, they're still developing the capacity to think with all the complexity afforded to adults.

It's critical for adults to understand this dynamic as we think about the spiritual development of children. Your children do not think about the world in the same ways you do. In their most formative years, children interpret the world categorically: good and bad, black and white, right and wrong. So if a six-year-old hears over and over that they are a "sinner," do you know what they internalize?

I'm bad. I'm not welcome. I'm worthless.

Who could blame them? Sin is terrible, and they lack the nuance to understand the complexity of living in the tension between sinner *and* saint.

In almost every teacher training I've done to date, I talk about the difference between what is *true* and what is *helpful*. Nowhere does this ring truer than in how we think about teaching children. Something may be accurate, but we also need to ask ourselves if it genuinely helps or hinders the audience. Another way to say this is, "It's not helpful if it's not helping." If a concept doesn't clarify but only confuses our children, then it is not actually helpful. I may be really jazzed about quantum mechanics, but it is not helpful to teach it to first graders.

Similarly, we need to teach children the Bible truthfully in ways that are also genuinely helpful.

So while it will be entirely appropriate to introduce upper elementary children to the sinner-saint paradigm, what children need to hear in the early years is that God delights in them. Of course, we still talk about sin with children before the age of eleven. It would be foolish to hide this from them, as it is foundational to the mercy of God and the work of Christ. However, we major on what God majors in. He delights in us. He freely chooses to love us at great cost to himself.

Feelings of Safety

Jesus told the Pharisees, in the presence of the disciples, "Let the little children come to me and do not hinder them, for to such belongs the kingdom of heaven" (Matthew 19:14). This passage comes in the context of a wide-ranging conversation on everything from divorce to riches. While we don't know specifically what Jesus meant by "hinder," we can broadly conclude that it meant anything that keeps a child from coming to Jesus. How might we invite children to Jesus instead of hindering them by our presentation of the gospel?

1. We can show children that Jesus is safe and trustworthy.

In a later chapter, we'll explore Maslow's Hierarchy of Needs. Through it, we'll learn that basic needs such as food, shelter, and safety precede our ability to trust and build relationships. Most of us ask the question, "Do I feel safe with you?" before we're willing to trust. Your children do the same. You want them to do this. It is their God-given impulse to help them steer clear of danger.

Now, don't hear what I'm not saying. God has provided the ultimate safety for his children.[4] There is nothing about God that is unsafe for those who have

---

4. Psalm 23:1–6; 91:1–2; Romans 8:37–39.

faith in Christ. My concern is not to change how the Bible presents God to our children. My concern surrounds the people who teach our young children about God—pastors, Sunday school teachers, and parents.

One Sunday school curriculum used by tens of thousands of churches world-wide this year asked teachers to lead pre-K and kindergarten students through the "sinner's prayer" every single Sunday. Many models of child discipleship are built on what is known as the Romans Road, which is a creative walk through the book of Romans to explain the salvific work of Christ. The first step of the Road is Romans 3:23: "For all have sinned and fall short of the glory of God." The second step is Romans 6:23: "For the wages of sin is death."

Both of these verses in Romans are profitable for teaching, and yet…we can do better to honor the full breadth of how God tells his own story. Our churches and families need disciple-makers who know that Genesis 1–2 is about so much more than the number of days it took to make the world. It's about the delight of God in his creation and in his people. The first and most primary fact about us is that we are worth delighting in simply because God chooses to.

Against this backdrop, children learn that God is safe and trustworthy. In coming to understand the character of God's delight, they'll be compelled by wonder, not guilt, to pursue a relationship with God.

2. It's about his love, not our sin.

A second way we can hinder children is by hardly speaking of sin. If this seems to contradict the first point, hold your question for just a moment. Just as in most things, there's a tendency to find ourselves at the extremes. Today, some mainline denominations and progressive parachurch organizations have virtually removed sin from their vocabulary. It seems too narrow-minded and exclusionary. They claim the way of Jesus is love, not limits.

I understand the impulse of these institutions to affirm God's love for the world. However, if we erase teaching about sin from children's discipleship, then what exactly do our kids need Jesus for? There are many teachers in the world who are glad to tell you how to live a good life and require far less of your time and attention. What sin tells our children is that they do not simply need another good teacher (although Jesus is that!). Instead, they need something more.

Principally, our children need to know that God loves them. Second, they need to know that God sees their biggest problem and loves them enough to provide a solution: Jesus's life of obedience, death for sinners, and resurrection.

One of my favorite modern hymns is "How Deep the Father's Love for Us." One of the lines, speaking of the crucifixion, sings, "It was my sin that held him there." This line is beautiful, as it highlights the work of Christ to save us through his humiliation and death on the cross. However much I appreciate this hymn, this line steals some of the glory of what Jesus did on the cross. In our church, we have substituted the line "It was *his love* that held him there." Yes, Jesus died for our sins, but what empowered him to do so was not our sin. Instead, it was his love.

Jesus says in John 10:17-18, "For this reason the Father loves me, because I lay down my life that I may take it up again. No one takes it from me, but I lay it down of my own accord." No one took Jesus's life from him. He did not lose it; he gave it in love for his people.

As we conclude this chapter, know this: Your children need more than the knowledge of God's delight in them. They need to be surrounded by people who embody the goodness of the gospel of delight. Those who've experienced the delight of God become less anxious because they aren't trying to impress anyone or control any outcomes—they already have the acceptance they need and understand that God is fully in charge of all our days. Those who know delight are less judgmental because they know that even though they deserve judgment, God chose them. We might say that those who have experienced the delight of God know the way of Jesus: showing kindness, rejoicing in the truth, bearing all things, hoping all things, enduring all things.

CHAPTER 5

Discipling Humility

Confession sends a crucial message to our children. It reminds them that, yes, my parents are imperfect, but they are deadly earnest about following Christ, about wanting to change, and about doing things God's way. Failure to confess our faults sends the opposite message. "My parents talk much about Christ, but following him is not really that important to them. They don't walk the talk. They tell us to do one thing, but they do the other. And when they fail, they go on as if it doesn't matter."

WILLIAM P. FARLEY

I spend every Tuesday night at a Samson Society meeting. It's sort of like Alcoholics Anonymous for men struggling with sexual brokenness. Vulnerability around this topic is rare but beautiful.

It's common for men to come to the group for the first time in a moment of crisis. Their wife just uncovered their secret and now their marriage is in trouble. Their employer found pornography on their work computer. It's almost the same set of stories every single time.

What I appreciate about this group is that all of us, whether it was one day ago or fifteen years ago, hit rock bottom. Our addiction became too much for us to handle or hide. We all experienced the frailty of being human, and instead of making audacious promises of "trying harder next time" and "never doing that again," we found the humility to confront our sin and move toward what we really needed: other men to walk alongside us and nearness to God.

For years, I had simply copied Adam and Eve's ill-fated attempts at hiding. What began as curiosity in high school blossomed into a full-scale addiction that followed me through college and into seminary. I learned to hide from even my closest friends. I put on the mask of an upstanding, responsible spiritual leader but, in the background, numbed the pain of shame and disappointment. In some ways, the hiding was hardwired into my body. Even the most sanctified of saints will attempt the illusion of hiding until the very end. After all, our first parents (and every parent since) have shown us how to do it.

Every man who has walked through the doors of Samson Society in the past few years has received a heavy dose of what David Zahl termed "high anthropology."[1] Don't be thrown off by the word *anthropology*. We are not about to get all academic here. Anthropology is simply a word to describe how we view what it means to be human.

High anthropology is, in many ways, normal for American families. We expect an enormous amount of success from our children. We believe we can achieve anything we set our minds to. If you do have the fortune of achieving a set of expectations, then high anthropology simply moves the bar one notch higher next time. We are never done achieving. To quote an earlier chapter, we believe we are only worthy inasmuch as we are useful.

In elementary school, I tested into the "gifted and talented" program. We

---

1. David Zahl, *Low Anthropology* (Brazos Press, 2022).

were supposed to receive additional resources to challenge us to reach our potential. I think there is plenty of legitimacy to programs like this. However, what I received was shame. In tenth grade, I struggled in my math class. I had hit a wall and did not know where to go. I can remember the teacher handing out grades midway through the quarter. I had a C. She looked at me disapprovingly as she set the paper on my desk while pointing to one word in parentheses next to my name: *gifted*. Was the label supposed to shield me from adversity? Was I allowed to struggle? In her eyes, I was supposed to be the student who did not give her a hard time, who was easy, and who sailed through school with no headwinds. But that was not the case. High anthropology had gotten the best of me.

I was the best of the best in my regular class, but once I was labeled as gifted, I was just ordinary, a below-average gifted student in a sea of students achieving at much higher levels. Two of my children are in such a program right now. They are much smarter than me, but it still terrifies the living daylights out of me that it will stir a similar anxiety inside of them.

Why Humility?

Books are limited in size, and so I can't write a chapter on every character trait I'd love to see developed in children. So why choose humility? My reason is twofold. First, humility is one of the clearest and most discernible character traits of Jesus. Second, from humility flows nearly every character trait we could hope to see in a disciple of Jesus.

The Example of Jesus

From the moment of his birth, Jesus taught humility through his actions as he was born into the humblest of circumstances. He was laid in a manger, a crib that doubled as a feeding trough for animals. His first visitors were humble shepherds.[2]

As Jesus began to perform miracles in Galilee, his fame spread throughout the region. Many flocked to him, some desiring to be healed, while others were simply curious. Jesus repeated the instruction after many of his miracles: Tell no one what you have seen. This humble request reflects a deeply held desire that he be valued for who he was and not merely his usefulness. He didn't heal others to increase his (or their) popularity but because healing is part of who he is.

After his miraculous feeding of the 5,000, some wanted to make Jesus their king. Such popularity and praise would have tempted or corrupted most people. But Jesus ignored the influence of the crowds, opting instead to be alone.[3]

On another occasion, Jesus rode triumphantly into Jerusalem. The crowds shouted words of praise, spreading their cloaks and tree branches before him.[4] However, Jesus chose this occasion to ride upon a donkey, a recognized messianic symbol of humility.[5]

Jesus demonstrated humility when he took the role of a servant in washing his disciples' feet. While washing, Jesus reflected on his own submission to the Father: "A servant is not greater than his master, nor is a messenger greater than the one who sent him" (John 13:16).

Finally, in his hours of greatest suffering, Jesus subjected himself to the Father. And in perhaps his greatest act of humility, Jesus allowed himself to be hung upon the cross. Some of his last words, in reference to the criminals hanging on either side, embody his humility: "Father, forgive them, for they know not what they do" (Luke 23:34).

---

2. Luke 2:7–20.
3. John 6:15.
4. Matthew 21:8–9.
5. Zechariah 9:9.

Jesus's life is laced with humility. Those who follow him, who sit at his feet, cannot help but be covered in the dust of their humble rabbi.

The Fruit of Humility

To this point, I have failed you in this chapter by not providing a definition of humility. But instead of a definition, it might be better for us to look at the fruit of a life lived in humility.

Tim Keller once wrote,

> C.S. Lewis in *Mere Christianity* makes a brilliant observation about gospel-humility at the very end of his chapter on pride. If we were to meet a truly humble person, Lewis says, we would never come away from meeting them thinking they were humble. They would not be always telling us they were a nobody (because a person who keeps saying they are a nobody is actually a self-obsessed person). The thing we would remember from meeting a truly gospel-humble person is how much they seemed to be totally interested in us.[6]

Isn't that the type of people we want our children to be? Isn't that the type of people we long to know? The organization CliftonStrengths has identified this character trait with what they refer to as *woo*.[7] You've likely met people who have this indescribably irresistible characteristic. We may call it the *woo factor*. We flock to people like this. They command the room—not in a domineering way but because everyone knows they genuinely care. People with high woo all have one thing in common—humility: the capacity to be less worried about what people think of us and the ability to think more about the needs, desires, and concerns of others.

---

6. Keller, *The Freedom of Self-Forgetfulness: The Path to True Christian Joy* (10Publishing, 2012) 31–32.
7. "An Introduction to the Woo® CliftonStrengths Theme," CliftonStrengths, Gallup, accessed July 9, 2024, https://www.gallup.com/cliftonstrengths/en/252359/woo-theme.aspx.

Even though Jesus could have commanded legions of angels at any moment, even though he could have seized earthly authority whenever he wanted, he instead "emptied himself, by taking the form of a servant, being born in the likeness of men" (Philippians 2:7). Why? So that he could show that he is totally interested in us. So that we would see ourselves in him. So that he could come to live the life we live and "give his life as a ransom for many" (Mark 10:45).

When we become truly interested in others, the fruit of the Spirit is formed in us. Just as a weight lifter only grows stronger through more repetitions of the same exercise, so the fruit of humility grows stronger through repetitions of looking to the needs of others as we see Jesus sacrificing for our needs. We cannot build and maintain healthy relationships with others if the fruit of humility, borne of the Spirit, is not growing within us: love, joy, peace, patience, kindness, generosity, faithfulness, gentleness, and self-control.

Leading Our Children in Humility

Humility is unnatural for children. To be sure, it isn't all that natural for adults either. Our natural tendency is selfishness. Adam thought it would be better to protect himself by hiding from God. Cain believed that killing his brother would solve his problems. Abraham wanted to hit the easy button and used Hagar to take the fastpass on his wait for a child. To overcome selfishness and move toward humility, our children need two very simple things: Jesus and us.

Paul writes,

> Therefore if you have any encouragement from being united with Christ, if any comfort from his love, if any common sharing in the Spirit, if any tenderness and compassion, then make my joy complete by being like-minded, having the same love, being one in spirit and of one mind. Do nothing out of selfish ambition or vain conceit.

Rather, in humility value others above yourselves, not looking to your own interests but each of you to the interests of the others (Philippians 2:1-4 NIV).

Notice Paul placing the indicative (what is true about God) before the imperative (our expected response). We can only be like-minded, loving, humble people who look to the interests of others because we are united with Christ and share in the Spirit. Rankin Wilbourne helpfully comments,

> Against the prevailing mindset of our day—you are what you make of yourself—union with Christ tells you that you can discover your real self only in relation to the One who made you. You are not, you cannot be, self-made. Union with Christ tells you that you can only understand who you are in communion with God and others. And that is a wildly countercultural claim.[8]

To agree with such a countercultural claim requires that we do countercultural things. Walking with our rabbi, Jesus, day after day is abnormal. It requires our children to see, feel, and be captivated by the delight of Jesus in them. Only then will they be able to turn to others and extend the kindness of humility.

The second thing our children need is us. We cannot expect our children to learn what they cannot see. God uses adults—and specifically parents—to shape the character of children. Like it or not, you are discipling your children in something. They watch you. They pick up little bits of information from how you spend your time and how you interact with others. If people are basically a means to an end for you, your kids will likely feel the same. But if they see you consistently looking to the interests of others, and they see that same character in Jesus, they, too, will be drawn to do the same.

This reality is reflected in the writer of Hebrews:

---

8. Rankin Wilbourne, *Union With Christ: The Way to Know and Enjoy God* (David C. Cook, 2016), 135.

> Therefore, since we are surrounded by so great a cloud of witnesses,
> let us also lay aside every weight, and sin which clings so closely,
> and let us run with endurance the race that is set before us, look-
> ing to Jesus, the founder and perfecter of our faith, who for the joy
> that was set before him endured the cross, despising the shame, and
> is seated at the right hand of the throne of God (Hebrews 12:1-2).

Parents, you are a part of that cloud of witnesses for your children. Because you model the humility of Jesus, they can more easily lay aside the weight of cultural expectations and sin and look to Jesus, who endured the cross—the ultimate display of humility.

A Word of Caution

Later in this book, we'll do a 5,000-foot flyover of the basics of child development. However, for now, it is important to remind you of a developmental milestone, as it relates to humility. Until around the age of seven, children are egocentric, which means they have a hard time seeing the world through other people's eyes. This is actually a remarkable gift for young children. The vulnerabilities of early childhood require children to use whatever awareness they have to protect themselves.

I often interact with parents of children in this developmental stage who bemoan the fact that their children are selfish and only concerned with themselves. Certainly, we want to encourage children to move out of this stage as their brains and bodies develop, but we can do little to rush this process. Children will not express humility, compassion, and empathy in the same way as adults. For this reason, young children need understanding adults who know that their lack of humility is not a problem to fix but a process to enter. Continue to teach children of the humility of Jesus. Model humility for them. Remain patient. Pray with and for them. This stage, too, will pass.

CHAPTER 6

Discipling Behavior

I spent a lot of time at the grocery store growing up. My dad worked long hours, and so we went *everywhere* with my mom. Everywhere. And we went grocery shopping *a lot*.

To this day, my mom still makes daily trips to Publix, likely more for the social experience than anything else. For some reason, planning, making a list, checking it twice, and going to the store—say, once a week—is not a skill set my family inherited.

At the store, my mom was the master of saying "no" to treats. It wasn't that we never had candy in the house or that my mom was stingy about sugar, but the creativity she employed to deny our requests for candy was admirable. Now that I am a parent, I understand. Mom, I'm sorry for all the badgering.

One of her favorite techniques to diffuse our nagging was to inform us that the rows of candy at the checkout were actually *not* for purchase. Instead, they were for *smelling*. We believed her for a long time. Can you imagine waiting in line behind us while my brother and I put our grimy hands on every piece of candy, shoving it as close to our nasal passages as possible before putting it back on the shelf? The 1980s. What a time to be alive!

One afternoon after school let out, we took our predictable daily trip to Publix. Like most days, I plotted out the sweet treat my heart would set its affections upon and how I would plead my case to acquire it. The answer, of course, was "no."

The request was for a large Jell-O cake—essentially Jell-O put in a bundt cake tin, turned upside down with whipped cream on top. It was lime green. It had a cherry on top. Chocolate sprinkles. Why do I still remember so many of these details? I would never eat it now. It sounds utterly disgusting.

My brother and I were five and six years old at the time, which in the 1980s meant we could roam the grocery store without supervision until my mom was done shopping. I walked by the Jell-O cake once. Then twice. Then three times. I looked around. Nobody was watching, and I was hungry.

I pried the lid off the Jell-O cake, stuck my head into the storage cooler, and took a big bite before carefully placing the lid back on and walking away as quickly as possible.

But someone was watching me. One of the employees must have known my mom due to our grocery store frequent-flier status. He found her and told her what he saw, and for the next three months, my allowance paid for that Jell-O cake.

My guess is you could tell similar stories about your own children. Children are born with an uncontrollable impulse to sin.[1] It is a part of their nature to rebel. Paul writes in Romans 3:23 that all of us "have sinned and fall short of the glory of God." It is one of the strange consequences of being human that we exchange the joy of obedience for the misery of sin.

---

1. Psalm 51:5.

In my work as a children's pastor, I often talk to parents who are stunned the first time their children misbehave, throw tantrums, or lie to their face. It can seem as though the innocent angel they brought home from the hospital has morphed into a serial killer overnight.

The Bible speaks plenty to parents about the importance of disciplining children in their behavior. Here's a small sample:

> Train up a child in the way he should go; even when he is old he will not depart from it (Proverbs 22:6).

> Children, obey your parents in the Lord, for this is right. "Honor your father and mother" (this is the first commandment with a promise), "that it may go well with you and that you may live long in the land." Fathers, do not provoke your children to anger, but bring them up in the discipline and instruction of the Lord (Ephesians 6:1-4).

> Children, obey your parents in everything, for this pleases the Lord. Fathers, do not provoke your children, lest they become discouraged (Colossians 3:20-21).

The Bible is abundantly clear on one thing: Parents bear the responsibility to help their children learn to behave in ways that honor and uphold Jesus's call:

> "Love the Lord your God with all your heart and with all your soul and with all your mind." This is the first and greatest commandment. And the second is like it: "Love your neighbor as yourself." All the Law and the Prophets hang on these two commandments (Matthew 22:36-40 NIV).

As clear as the Bible is on the *what* of discipling the behavior of children, it is far less clear on the *how*. You won't find instructions for what to do when your rogue six-year-old licks the Jell-O cake in the middle of Publix. However, here are some postures and lessons I have found helpful in guiding my own children at home and the thousands of children who have come through our church.

Obedience to God

If you'll remember, earlier in this book, we talked about needing a *why* to pursue the things of God. Our kids are no different. They are only human, after all. When it comes to obedience, children need to develop a heart-level conviction for why they are to obey their parents and others in authority. Let's observe once more some passages about obedience to authority.

> Children, obey your parents in the Lord, for this is right (Ephesians 6:1).

> Children, obey your parents in everything, for this pleases the Lord (Colossians 3:20).

These nearly identical passages make it crystal clear that obedience to parents is obedience to the Lord. Why is obedience such a central theme for those who honor the Lord?

In the book of Philippians, Paul quotes the "Christ hymn" (Philippians 2:6-11). He pleads that they might have the same mind that was in Christ Jesus (verse 5). Having this mind, they will then be able to fulfill his hope for them: that they may live "in a manner worthy of the gospel" (Philippians 1:27 NIV).

The Christ hymn is one of the earliest known professions of faith. It is the story of salvation in Christ in three parts: self-emptying (incarnation), obedience (death on a cross), and exaltation (resurrection and ascension).

Through the incarnation, Jesus willingly took on human form and limitations. Through his humble obedience, Jesus serves as a counterexample to Adam and Eve in the Garden of Eden, who, for their own selfish gain, grasp at likeness to God. In his self-emptying, Jesus sees equality with God not as something to be used for his own advantage but as an offering for others. This desire results in radical obedience and service to others, even suffering and death on a cross.

In the exaltation, God celebrates the self-denying service embodied in Christ's death. The one who came as servant is now proclaimed Lord of all. Christ's authority to be called Lord comes not only from his exaltation by God through the resurrection and ascension but through his obedience. Because of his obedience, he who did not grasp at likeness to God is given a title that proclaims that very likeness.

Therefore, Paul suggests that incorporation into the body of Christ demands humility and obedience of the type demonstrated by Jesus, both for children and for adults. This is the way his disciples gain the "mind of Christ." This humility is not humiliation, nor is the obedience blind. Rather, they are expressions of faith and trust in the gracious and loving character of God.

How do our children get this "mind of Christ"? They walk closely with their rabbis. They sit at their feet and learn. They become dust-covered disciples.

Hear this: What we do when we "disciple behavior" is really discipleship of character. We want them to obey, but only because it is a part of taking on the mind of Christ. Character is a Crock-Pot set of qualities, slowly formed over long periods of time as God himself disciples our children.

As our children experience the honesty of Jesus, they, too, will desire honesty.

As our children see the gentleness of Jesus, they, too, will grow to be gentle people.

As our children see the truthfulness of Jesus, they, too, will value truth.

No single lesson, list of rules, or devotional will give our children the mind of Christ. It is, instead, a gift of the Spirit, cultivated by continually modeling what it looks like to pursue Christ and putting our children in the places where God has already promised to work.

Be Generous in Your Assessments

We cannot see our children's hearts. While they are sinful, it is not easy to distinguish between immaturity, emotional dysregulation, and consciously chosen sin. We should never discipline our children for acting in accord with their developmental age. Parents raising disciples from a posture of humility bear with children as they grow in maturity and never discipline their children for simply being children. To parent in this way requires an enormous amount of self-awareness and a lifetime of cultivation, but it is worth it because it is truly a gift to your family.

Now, this is not to say that we should simply let our children off the hook. There are plenty of times our children sin, know they've sinned, and need to be corrected. After all, Jeremiah 17:9 applies to all people, children and adults alike: "The heart is deceitful above all things, and desperately sick; who can understand it?"

However, some knowledge and understanding of humanity goes a long way toward engaging in appropriate measures of corrective action. Here are a few keys.

1. Maintain a non-anxious presence when your children misbehave.

It can be easy to allow our surprise, embarrassment, hurt, and shame to overwhelm the situation. Breathe. Unclench your fists. Loosen your jaw. A well-regulated body can think and act clearly. A well-regulated parent is a safe person for a child to be with, no matter what they've done. Anxiety and calm are both transferable emotions, meaning we can de-escalate another person's worry simply by not getting worked up ourselves.

2. Recognize your own triggers.

Nothing quite ignites my bad tendencies like a messy kid's bedroom.[2]

---

2. If this sounds familiar, yes, I did reference my children's unsanitary bedrooms earlier in this book. May this forever serve as a marker of my stage of parenting while writing this book.

Clothes and toys scattered about can feel like the end of the world. Why? My wife can walk into the same room and see signs of life, love, and kids being kids. But for me, it feels like I'm being personally attacked. It feels like my children are trying to send some cryptic message of disrespect. Then I began listening to the disrespectful tone coming from my demand of "Boys, upstairs, right now! For the millionth time, clean your room!" I didn't hear the kindness of Jesus; I heard the voice of my grandfather, who demanded the same things of my mother, who then demanded the same things of me. Generational sin played out right from the top of our staircase.

Just as the simple pull of a rifle's trigger unleashes a magnitude of power far greater than the motion of your finger, so our triggers prove that something much more significant lies hidden beneath the surface. It's a check-engine light, and one you should not ignore. A counselor friend of mine who knows me well reminds me from time to time, "If it feels hysterical, it's probably historical." Remain suspicious of your outsized responses. They're likely a lot less about the goal of discipling your children and more about the emotional baggage you carry.

3. Stay curious.

Ask questions of situations before jumping to conclusions. See the strong emotions around the behavior. See your child's heart. One of my favorite college professors used to say, "The problem with the problem is not the problem. The problem with the problem is the strong emotions around the problem."

Rarely do parents make situations worse by moving slowly. Plenty of relationships sustain damage from those involved feeling rushed to judgment. For our family's messy-room situation, once we became curious and began asking questions of our children, we learned the origin of the issue lay in a shared space. We have a large bonus room upstairs that doubled as our boys' bedroom and the playroom for all four kids, including our youngest two girls. Every other day, someone got in trouble for leaving the room messy, and since it was the boys' bedroom, I blamed them 90 percent of the time (they would say 100 percent).

Only when we became curious did the situation change. They shared with us that it wasn't them who left everything messy. It was the girls, who were three and six at the time and simply doing what three- and six-year-old girls do…making messes and not cleaning up. We apologized and asked them to help us find a solution. We did. The boys moved to a new room. The messes all but disappeared. Everything changed because we became curious about their experience and asked for their input and for their forgiveness.

Curiosity is a kindness that costs us nothing and gives the dignity of Jesus to our children.

4. Context matters.

Ask simple questions such as, What time of day is it? When did they last eat? Is this a new experience? Has something unexpected happened? Sometimes your child is simply having a hard time not giving you a hard time. They're hungry. They're nervous. It's past their bedtime. We become grace-filled parents when we remember that our children do not exist in a vacuum. They, too, have triggers and limits.

Atypical situations cause children to do atypical things. Extraordinary parents know this and lead their children in context. To do so requires an exceptional level of restraint and an unusual experience of God's grace to us when we, too, do atypical things in the face of atypical situations.

As I reflect on these four concepts, I can't help but think this is the way I want to be treated by others. This is the way God treats me. It's the way I want my children to treat others. If all those things are true, then I cannot expect from them what I don't model.

Mean-spirited, angry, rude children typically come from the homes of parents who are mean-spirited, angry, and rude. Behavior is a parroted, conditioned response to the world.

Likewise, gracious, kind, and generous children typically come from the homes of gracious, kind, and generous parents. More often than not, these parents have been covered in the dust of their rabbi, Jesus.

Don't Assume the Worst

There's a first time for everything. Last night, as I taught a group of fifty children at our church, I was hit in the face by a full water bottle. Totally blindsided. I did not see it coming at all. You could have heard a pin drop in the room as everyone awaited my response. A few kids called out the name of the offender.

Time seemed to slow down as I recognized the gravity of my next few words. I could have been harsh and humiliated the child in front of everyone. I could have gone to self-pity and shut the lesson down. Instead, the Lord reminded me of one of my guiding principles when working with children: Don't assume the worst. Maybe the bottle slipped out of the child's hand. Certainly he didn't mean to hit me in the face.

And so, I responded with a laugh, "Well, I guess there's a first time for everything!" After the lesson, I was able to talk privately with the child and repair the relationship. This skill of assuming the best about children's behavior has been cultivated over the years of parenting and pastoring. Part of that cultivation has been the practice of these four simple beliefs:

1. For every worst-case scenario, there's an equally likely best-case scenario.
Choose to imagine the latter. Our proclivity to drift toward worst-case scenarios is a natural fear response to protect us from danger. Imagining best-case scenarios, therefore, is a disciplined practice and pursuit of God's grace.

2. Remember, your children did not wake up and think, *How can I make someone's day horrible?*

Nobody (except a few psychopaths) wants to ruin someone else's day. Instead, it's our abnormal sinful nature that makes us self-serving. Sin is the enemy, not our children.

3. Everyone is doing the best they can with the resources they have.

Your children lack the impulse control you possess. They lack the life experience and social skills you have gained. They don't see the world with the maturity that you do. Choose to believe that they are doing the best they can with the resources they have.

4. Suspend your privilege to believe the worst until you ask questions.

To believe the worst is a form of hatred. You don't have the right to hate anyone or anyone's actions without a more well-rounded picture of the situation. Ask questions before making assessments.

How God Responds to Our Sin

The way God cares for his children in the first book of the Bible gives us a beautiful example of how parents should respond to their children's sin.

Notice, after Adam and Eve rebel, God moves toward them. He does not give them the shame-filled silent treatment. He does not isolate them in time-out. Instead, God seeks them out.

Even when "the man and his wife hid themselves from the presence of the LORD God among the trees of the garden" (Genesis 3:8), God called to them. God did not play a game of chicken, waiting to smoke the first couple out of hiding. It is not in God's nature to wait passively. Instead, what we see in Genesis 3 is the beginning of a pattern repeated throughout the Bible. People mess up, try to hide, and yet God graciously pursues them. Moses, David, Jonah, and more were all "hiders." And yet the Bible repeats hundreds of times some variation of what the writer of Hebrews says: "No creature is hidden from his sight" (Hebrews 4:13). Perhaps no other place in the Bible displays this as clearly as the parable of the prodigal son.

In this famous parable, both sons disobey the father, and yet he moves toward them in the particular ways each one needed in the moment. For the younger son, this meant confronting the lie of "I am no longer worthy to be called your son" (Luke 15:21) with a regal reception of belonging. There was no correction or punishment. There was no "Go to your room, young man, and don't come out until I say so!" Instead, the father saw his hurting son and knew the path to healing was a warm embrace. This is a picture of a non-anxious father who placed relationship with his son above the opportunity to either vent his anger or administer judgment in the middle of a contextually complex situation.

Meanwhile, the older son refused to go near his father once he learned about the celebration of the one who "devoured" (Luke 15:30) his father's property. So the father left the party to remind him, "Son, you are always with me, and all that is mine is yours" (verse 31). Again, no correction or punishment. The father recognized his son's fear, which had boiled over into rage.

With a calm and well-regulated posture, the father does his best to lower the temperature. Again, he parents in context, seeing the circumstances surrounding this outburst were not normal. Atypical situations cause people to do atypical things. Extraordinary parents know this and parent in context. The words of my college professor ring true here: "The problem with the problem is not the problem. The problem with the problem is the strong emotions around the problem."

The father in Luke 15 is a beautiful picture of our God, who draws near to his people when they least deserve it. Dane Ortlund summarizes God's heart for his people: "The sins of those who belong to God open the floodgates of his heart of compassion for us…It is not our loveliness that wins his love. It is our unloveliness."[3]

Be a parent who moves with compassion toward your child's heart when they feel unlovely. When their shame tells them they are unwanted and unworthy, show them they are important with your time, your words, and your body.

Next, notice that God calls Adam and Eve to understand what they've done by being curious. He asks them questions of which he already knows the answers. Does this strike you as odd? God already knows what they have done. He saw the whole thing. He doesn't need to gather more details to piece together the crime scene.

> "Who told you that you were naked? Have you eaten of the tree of which I commanded you not to eat?" (Genesis 3:11). Then the LORD God said to the woman, "What is this that you have done?" (Genesis 3:13).

Adam and Eve are far from honest in their answers, opting instead to shift the blame. Even still, God maintains a posture of curiosity—not for his benefit but for the instruction of these first humans and all who would come after them.

A parent's job is not to back their children into a corner, asking as many questions as necessary to garner a confession of guilt. Instead, we ask just the right amount of non-anxious questions to help our children take the next step in living out the call to love God and their neighbor.

Here are some examples of poorly worded questions and alternatives:

Instead of: Why did you do that?

Try: I saw/heard you _____. I'm curious, what was going on inside your heart when you did that?

---

3. Dane Ortlund, *Gentle and Lowly* (Crossway, 2020), 75.

Instead of: What were you thinking?

Try: I know you don't normally behave like this. I wonder, is there something going on beneath the surface you haven't told us?

Instead of: Why do you always do this?

Try: Sometimes we do things we don't want to do without even thinking about it. Can I help you overcome this?

Next, notice that God does not rescue his children from all the consequences of their sin. He does, however, protect them from the worst consequences. The serpent is cursed, and the end of his life is foretold with the ominous statement that one of Eve's offspring will "bruise [his] head" (Genesis 3:15). Even though their sin deserves death, God is merciful toward his children. He does not give them the full measure of their punishment.

Instead, he allows the natural consequences of their actions to play out. Eve will experience pain in childbirth; both of them will act in ways to destroy their own relationship with each other; Adam's work will become frustrating and nearly impossible to accomplish. They can no longer live in the garden.

God could have made them eat a disgusting, rotten bowl of fruit. He could have made them do 1,000 push-ups. But these would have been abstract consequences. Instead, God allows the very basis of their existence—to be fruitful and multiply—to come under natural attack.

God carefully chooses his words when he speaks to his children, who are made in his image. God curses the serpent and the ground, but he does not curse Adam and Eve. Parents would do well to learn from this example. The old adage "Hate the sin, not the sinner" is perhaps most needed for those closest to us. While we may not hate our children, our words can communicate differently. Speak gently and matter-of-factly to your children. Pray that God would set a guard over your mouth to bless and guide your children through difficult moments.

After all, what is the goal of discipline? Is it to make our children pay? Is it to strike fear in their hearts so they won't do it again? Perhaps it's to satisfy our own desire for justice. If these are our goals, we need to find our way back to the heart of the gospel—that God bore our sin in his body on the cross so that we would not get what we deserve but see that God really does actually love us more than we could ever hope or imagine. When our children see that kind of love reflected in their parents, they are more likely to resonate with the character of God, who does the same, in exponentially greater measure.

Finally, notice that God doesn't shame Adam and Eve, even though they were experiencing shame. Instead, he covers their shame. In Genesis 3:21, God has not forgotten Adam's new fear of nakedness, exposed in 3:10. Instead, Moses records, "The LORD God made for Adam and for his wife garments of skins and clothed them." God covered their shame.

While guilt is the emotion that says, "I have done something wrong," shame is much more powerful. Shame believes, "*I* am wrong." Shame says, "There is something fundamentally flawed within *me*. I am unacceptable."

Guilt can be forgiven, but shame must be covered. Forgiveness is far easier than covering for one simple reason: Covering shame requires you to see the other person's suffering.

God saw Adam and Eve's suffering in this new, naked reality. It would be impossible for them to take steps toward healing because they now looked at their bodies and believed there was something fundamentally flawed about their appearance. Adam and Eve could have, over time, figured out how to make their own clothing, but it would have simply been an extension of their pattern of hiding. Their shame would not have been covered by another, and shame that is covered by someone who sees your suffering is healing.

And so God made garments for them and clothed them. Adam and Eve did not ask for the garments, but God saw their suffering and, in his unmerited kindness, covered their shame.

Parents, forgiveness is great. It is a worthy goal of relational healing. But all of us know the icky, sticky feeling of shame that glues itself to our hearts. Consider the ways you can cover your children's shame:

- Write a note for their lunch box that reminds them that they are a valuable part of the family.

- Have a night at the dinner table where everyone shares one thing they love about one another.

- Go out of your way to show up for something your child didn't think you would be there for.

Finally, notice that God loves his children too much to allow them to make the same mistakes again. He put boundaries in place to prevent Adam and Eve from suffering worse consequences in the future. They can no longer live in the garden. God places cherubim and a flaming sword to guard the tree of life. Boundaries should not be confused with punishments. Boundaries are gifts that keep us from our worst impulses. Punishments shame children into hiding their worst impulses so as to avoid future punishments. Boundaries exist to give our children breathing room so their affections for God and their love for others can grow.

If you've been a parent for more than a few months, you know that learning lessons is an iterative process. While we shouldn't handcuff our children, it is an act of love to see their tendencies and protect them from becoming the worst versions of themselves. If you have multiple children, boundaries will look different for each child. It won't "seem fair" that a boundary exists for one child and not another. That's okay.

What About Punishment?

A lot has been made in the past few years of the so-called gentle parenting movement. It can be difficult to pin down exactly what this movement involves. It's all over social media, so you can be sure there are many caricatures of it. One internet search of the phrase, and the next three months of your algorithm will include an endless stream of posts.

The basic premise is that we should see our children as essentially good. It tends to move away from clear definitions of sin and, for some, involves an outright denial of sin. The solution to raising well-adjusted children, the movement asserts, is to minimize or altogether eliminate punitive elements of parenting. The real secret sauce, the movement claims, is connection. When your children struggle or misbehave, they need to reconnect with their parents and be reminded of their goodness. Punishment merely severs the relationship further and leads children to rebel or simply learn to hide better next time.

I have friends on both sides of the aisle on this issue. As I write this, I'm also preparing to speak on a panel alongside several well-known gentle parenting experts. I'm also preparing to speak at one of the most traditional, conservative parenting conferences at the end of next month. I want to be notoriously hard to pin down on this issue because I don't think either side has it right. As with most two-sided arguments, people feel the need to take extreme positions so as to differentiate themselves from the others. I don't think that's healthy. Instead, we need to think more biblically and less culturally about punishment as a tool.

To begin, we need to recapture the word *gentle*. Dane Ortlund describes Jesus this way: "Meek. Humble. Gentle. Jesus is not trigger-happy. Not harsh, reactionary, easily exasperated. He is the most understanding person in the universe. The posture most natural to him is not a pointed finger but open arms."[4]

---

4. Dane Ortlund, "Jesus's 'About Me' Section," April 15, 2020, https://www.crossway.org/articles/jesuss-about
   -me-section/.

The apostle Paul exhorts us to "walk in a manner worthy of the calling to which you have been called, with all humility and gentleness, with patience, bearing with one another in love" (Ephesians 4:1-2).

Bear with one another. What a beautiful phrase. When we bear with someone, we don't always get what we want. The outcome can feel out of control. Bearing with one another is inconvenient and unnatural. It involves seeing, *really seeing* someone and what would best support their growth. And yet Paul tells us that those who are gentle cannot help but bear with one another in love.

What might bearing with our children look like? For me, it's looked like acknowledging that my children do not see the world the way I do. Literally everything children come into contact with, especially in the early years, is a first-time experience. As a forty-year-old, I am fluent in social and moral norms in most places I enter. My children are not. They're still learning what it means to be human.

A skill I want you to spend the rest of your parenting journey developing is to have eyes of wisdom to discern what is sin and what is simply a lack of social and moral fluency. You'll never get this perfect, but it will be one of the greatest gifts you can possibly give your family.

When we treat a lack of social or moral fluency as if it is sin, we destroy children's confidence and increase feelings of shame. Some children steal a candy bar because they know it's wrong but they still want the candy bar (even though it's just for smelling…remember). But some children think the candy is there to take because that's the way it is at school or home. They don't have a fully formed concept of what a store is yet.

Children growing in social and moral fluency do not need to be punished. They need support and someone to teach them skills. They need a non-anxious adult to guide them toward wisdom. But if a child is in sin and needs to be punished, Paul has some clear guidance for parents.

In his letter to the Galatians, Paul speaks directly to how we think about those who may need to be punished: "Brothers, if anyone is caught in any transgression, you who are spiritual should restore him in a spirit of gentleness" (Galatians 6:1-2).

Parents, the "anyone" at the beginning of the verse really does mean *anyone*. No exclusions. Your children should be restored in a spirit of gentleness—not only for their sake but for yours too.

Galatians 6:1 ends with this warning: "Keep watch on yourself, lest you, too, be tempted." When we have the privilege of restoring our children after a transgression, it can be an occasion for pride and anger. Watch yourself. Maintain a gentle posture.

God's default position toward his people is that of love and welcome in the face of their sin. This doesn't mean he never punishes. It would be foolish to claim that (see nearly the entire period of Israel's exile). However, the overwhelming biblical evidence suggests that God's purposes are to reclaim sinners in relationship.

A Word on Spanking

There's been more chatter on the internet about spanking than perhaps any other parenting topic out there. It's a hotbed for controversy, make no mistake about it. Many of us are pretty sure the Bible endorses spanking, but it still makes us a little uncomfortable. Some are a little too cozy with spanking as a go-to punishment.

Faithful Christians come down on either side of the debate over spanking. Some are in favor, and others are not. Many are undecided or in the middle. We can have fellowship with Christians on all areas of the spectrum. Spanking is not a theological issue of salvation. However, it is an issue of justice. How we choose to care for the most vulnerable people in our families is of utmost importance. So it is worth examining in some detail.

Let's take a look at what the Bible teaches about spanking. The vast majority of support for spanking as a biblical virtue comes from Proverbs 13:24: "Whoever spares the rod hates his son, but he who loves him is diligent to discipline him."

The image of the rod is important to this proverb, but not for the reason most might suspect. The rod here is similar to one that a shepherd may carry. The first readers would have been quite familiar with this imagery. Because of that, they would have seen the extension of this illustration with the son as the sheep and the parents as the shepherd.

Every time I teach this passage and set the scene as I just did, those listening usually assume that the rod is a weapon the shepherd uses to hit the sheep to get them to do what he wants them to do. But that is not the case at all.

First, we need to acknowledge that our understanding of discipline has been culturally conditioned. The first readers of Proverbs would have had a much broader understanding of discipline than we do.

Discipline was the umbrella term for instruction or teaching. Today, discipline (in the context of children) almost exclusively means punishment.

Second, the assumption that the rod was used by shepherds to hit sheep shows a lack of understanding of sheep farming. Here's what I mean…

Shepherds use rods to help their sheep go in the right direction with gentle nudges. The rod provides a sense of comfort and reassurance for the sheep that the shepherd has their best interests in mind and will not let them go astray. This is why Psalm 23:4 can say, "Your rod and your staff, they comfort me."

Suddenly, Proverbs 13:24 sounds very different from our culturally conditioned version. It is not punitive; it's pedagogical.

Now, you could imagine a scenario where the shepherd would use the rod to strike a sheep. Perhaps one sheep is trying to attack another and needs to be stopped. Perhaps they are about to fall off a cliff and are unresponsive to the shepherd's nudges. Maybe they are about to enter somewhere that presents an immediate danger, and the shepherd needs to suddenly stop them. Point being, yes—the rod can be used for striking (although for most of these situations, the staff would be used as it has a hook on the end to grab the sheep and yank him back).

Just ten chapters after Proverbs 13, we read this: "Do not withhold discipline from a child; if you strike him with a rod, he will not die. If you strike him with the rod, you will save his soul from Sheol" (Proverbs 23:13-14).

Notice the language shift of this second proverb: "He will not die...you will save his soul from Sheol." Sounds serious, right? So can the rod be used to strike a child? Yes, but only in the most dire life-and-death situations.

Not for refusing to pick up toys.

Not for talking back.

Not for embarrassing you in public.

I hate to make an argument from silence, but I do think it is curious that the New Testament never talks about spanking. Instead, when the New Testament writers discuss parenting, they do so with a warning for parents to not exasperate their children.[5]

I know many of you reading this have different convictions regarding spanking. How we discipline our children is what theologians call a third-tier issue; believers can respectfully hold differing opinions while not breaking fellowship. That being said, I want to leave you with this thought: Wherever you stand on spanking or any other method of discipline, be sure your convictions are grounded in a thorough examination of Scripture and not merely in pragmatism or tradition.

---

5. Colossians 3:20–21; Ephesians 6:4.

CHAPTER 7

Discipling the Body

My friends and I left the camp at midnight, climbed through the early morning hours, and arrived at the top of Horn Peak, just outside of Westcliffe, Colorado, an hour before sunrise. The air was dead silent, and the nearest streetlight was more than fifteen miles away. Stars popped from every corner of the sky—ones I'd never seen before and ones I'll likely never see again. As the sun rose, it almost seemed to make an audible noise against the dark and tranquil sky—as if it were peeling back the night for a new day to begin. The wind began to blow lightly as the temperature changed the barometric pressure ever so slightly. Little mountain critters—marmots—came out of their rock hiding places to look for any wildflowers that had emerged. In the distance, we saw a family of bighorn sheep beginning their morning walkabout.

As beautiful as this scene was, it is remarkably normal. It happens every morning on Horn Peak, but it felt like our group was attending a private viewing of the most spectacular sights the world has ever seen—God's beautiful creation on display for five twenty-year-old camp counselors. Perhaps this is what Abram experienced in Genesis 15 when God asked him to count the stars.

Last night, I went outside on the neighborhood streets of the dense suburban sprawl where our family lives just outside of Chattanooga. I carefully counted just over fifty stars as I listened to the semitrucks roaring by on the interstate just a quarter mile away. It was a crystal-clear night—not a cloud in sight.

I couldn't help but think of the exponentially greater message Abram received as he stared into the sky and God promised him descendants as numerous as the stars. Jeremiah would later recall the sky as having stars so numerous they could not be counted.[1] Not only did Abram see God's illustration that one night, but every night following, he was reminded of God's promise as he stared into the sky without the modern-day masking of streetlights.

This early morning Colorado hike happened in 2004. That summer, I joined a team of forty other college students from around the country to work at a summer camp for kids known as Snowridge. Some of us worked in the kitchen, others as low-ropes instructors, and still others (like me) had the unenviable job of living and sleeping in the cabins with groups of ten smelly twelve-year-old boys devoid of parental care for weeks at a time. The silver lining, though, was that we got every other week off from working at camp to do as we pleased. This, I now realize, was a consolation prize for the fact that our only compensation was a plane ticket and room and board. We were unpaid workers—likely the victims of several legal violations, but we had the time of our lives. Now, as an adult, I want to go back and tell my twenty-year-old self just how good he had it that summer!

---

1. Jeremiah 33:22.

Within an hour of the camp were more 13,000- and 14,000-foot mountains than we could climb. Class 5 white water rapids were within a thirty-minute drive. The first day we arrived at camp, I remember sitting with the other male counselors in my bunk as we agreed to not allow one another to waste a moment of this incredible opportunity. We kept that promise.

I'll always be thankful for my time at Snowridge for more than the beauty of the scenery. It was there I first discovered that God values more than my repentance and obedience. He values me and created me with a good mind and a good body. My worth is bound up in more than my salvation. The goal of life is not simply to earn a get-out-of-jail-free card. No, our lives have value because of all that God has saved us for!

That means a critical part of discipleship is discovering and enjoying God's delights in us as physical creatures. He created us with bodies bursting with the capacity to play, explore, imagine, and create!

The Power of Play

A recent landmark study funded by the LEGO Foundation and overseen by Kathy Hirsh-Pasek, PhD, a professor of psychology at Temple University and a senior fellow at the Brookings Institution, found that play is anything but optional when it comes to human development.[2]

One of their critical findings is that children, even as young as a few hours old, prefer to play. Initially, babies listen more intently to human voices than any other sound. Then they become interested in visually exploring their environment and later become fascinated by manipulating, moving, touching, tasting, and smelling anything they can get their hands on. Later, this drive toward play compels children to interact with a broader range of their environment.

---

2. "Learning Through Play: What the Science Says," Learning Through Play, LEGO Foundation, accessed July 10, 2024, https://learningthroughplay.com/explore-the-research/the-scientific-case-for-learning-through-play.

The study highlighted the work of other researchers—notably, the robust field of interconnected domains of learning. While play was once thought to be a bonus for humans of all ages, we now know that it's a part of a series of interconnected gears where development in one area can influence development in another. Physical exertion through play has a tremendous impact on later cognitive and social development.[3]

Working at Snowridge was a developmental incubator for me, in part, because of play. That early morning hike to the top of Horn Peak is just one example of many. In order to accomplish the hike, I needed the social skills to interact with and then dream with a group of people. One of us had to take the risk of suggesting the plan to others. I had to learn how to hike, what supplies I would need, and how to regulate my breathing (I grew up in oxygen-rich, sea-level Florida, after all!). We had to prepare for the unknown, take appropriate risks, and ask for help from more experienced people.

I saw this play out week after week at camp, not just on the nighttime Horn Peak hike. In my weeks as a counselor, I watched kids arrive at camp on Sunday, have a television and video game withdrawal on Monday, and then begin to play on Tuesday. By Friday, they were different children. They played for six days, and it brought out more of who God made them to be—wonderfully made, emotional, social people whom God delights in.

Play is the secret sauce when it comes to our development as God's children. The LEGO Foundation points to three crucial characteristics of play that enable deep learning: joy, meaning, and engagement. I don't know about you, but I hear a lot of the kingdom of God in those three words!

---

3. Lana Karasik, Catherine Tamis-LeMonda, and Karen Adolph, "Crawling and Walking Infants Elicit Different Verbal Responses from Mothers," *Developmental Science* 17, no. 3 (2014): 388–95. https://doi .org/10.1111/desc.12129.

The Power of Creating

Facebook launched on February 4, 2004—just three months before my time at Snowridge. I wrote this book in 2024, twenty years later, which may as well be a lifetime. Nobody had an iPhone in 2004 because they were still three years away. The camp had no televisions anywhere. The office had one computer, which we were allowed to use for ten minutes each week—barely enough time to write an email home to reassure our parents that we hadn't been eaten by a grizzly bear.

What did we do with our time? We talked, read, played, thought, prayed, listened, and wrote. *We moved from being consumers to being creators.* We took in the surroundings and imagined what we could do with them. We explored, we swam, we paddled, we wondered all summer at God's creation.

I'm not certain we can give our children any greater gift than the ability and space to wonder. When we allow wonder to creep into their imaginations, our children possess the superpower to create. Whether it is creativity with pen and pencil, wood and nails, shovels and dirt, or even the use of time, it connects them to the heart of God, who is known first and foremost as a creator. God builds, he listens, he speaks, he prays, he writes.

The first thing Moses tells us about God in the book of Genesis is that he created. The first thing we learn about ourselves is that we are made in his likeness. Ashlee Gadd notes in her book *Create Anyway*, "If God is the first artist—and we are a walking, breathing reflection of him—this means our desire to create is hereditary, a fundamental imprint of his Spirit in us."[4]

When God created Adam and Eve, he commissioned them to be co-creators. Genesis 2:15 recounts that after ensuring the Garden of Eden had adequate irrigation, God set Adam in the middle of it and told him to "work it and keep it." Can you imagine the wonder Adam awoke to every day? *This place is beautiful.*

---

4. Ashlee Gadd, *Create Anyway* (Bethany House, 2023), 29.

Where will I plant the next row of crops? What will I name this new swimmy thing? I know… "dolphin"!

Work it and *keep* it. This is still the call for God's people today. When we work and keep what God has made, we become captivated by the beauty of his handiwork and point others to the one who created all things.

God had other news for Adam. Adam was not simply a creator. He was also a consumer—but not the modern-day Walmart-shopper variety. He was called to steward his consumption. We could even say Adam was asked to moderate his consumption. When we steward, we become caretakers. We take responsibility for the possibilities of and embrace the limitations of God's gifts. We acknowledge that not all things that appear to be good are actually for our best.

God called Adam to this type of stewarded consumership in Genesis 2:16: "You may surely eat of every tree of the garden." God gave Adam license to consume that which is a good product of his creative work. But notice this: There are limits to this consumption. Genesis 2:17 reads, "But of the tree of the knowledge of good and evil you shall not eat." In other words, "Adam, you must moderate and limit your consumption. Only then will you truly flourish."

Today, our culture celebrates those who push boundaries and question the status quo. Some of this is good, as the work of being a creative is essentially a curiosity about our limitations. However, much of it is damaging. It crosses lines—good lines—that God has set for us.

If listening to God's wisdom does not guide our creation and consumption, then certainly the indicators are readily apparent. Our bodies know when we have crossed that line.

Surely the largest impediments to our children's creative capacity today are screens in all their varied forms—video games, smartphones, computers, and so on. It is not lost on me that the vast majority of our children will one day have jobs that necessitate them spending massive amounts of time in front of screens. I've spent no small amount of time in front of a screen while writing this book, after all!

The problem is not the screens but what we do with them. While the Bible provides no specific guidance on screen usage, we can glean some wisdom without even leaving the first few chapters of Genesis.

A recent University of Michigan study found that on average, kids play outside four to seven *minutes* a day but use screened devices four to seven *hours* each day.[5] That, ladies and gentlemen, is what we call insanity. Those numbers are about as out of balance as anyone can imagine.

What do kids do in front of these screens? I'm sure some small percentage of children use their screen time to create works of art in Adobe, but you know as well as I do that screens are consumption devices. Our screened devices have all the potential to create flourishing, and yet we use them to zone out and numb our God-given senses—senses necessary to create.

In his book *Glow Kids*, Nicholas Kardaras notes a study from the University of Tubingen that showed that over a twenty-year period, we have lost 1 percent of our sensory awareness every year. He said, "15 years ago people could distinguish 300,000 sounds; today many children can't go past 100,000. Twenty years ago the average subject could detect 250 shades of a particular color. Today the number is 130."[6] Our children's bodies are keeping the score of lives devoid of play, moderation, creativity, and engagement with the physical world.

Our refusal to heed Adam's call to moderation and creativity has resulted in all manner of chaos. This rebellion affects every part of our being…even our eyes and ears and, by proxy, our ability to create. When we don't create, we don't enjoy the fullness of what it means to be human. Cal Newport warns us in his book *Digital Minimalism*, "We should treat with great care any new technology

---

5. "There's a Reason They Call it the Great Outdoors," National Wildlife Foundation, 2010, https://www.nwf .org/~/media/PDFs/Be%20Out%20There/MindBodySpirit_FactSheet_May2010.ashx.
6. Nicholas Kardasis, *Glow Kids* (St. Martin's Press, 2017), 30.

that threatens to disrupt the ways in which we connect and communicate with others. When you mess with something so central to the success of our species, it's easy to create problems."[7]

Adam should have listened to Cal. So should we.

The Power of Fitness

Living at 10,000-foot elevation changes your body. You burn more calories, your body becomes more oxygen efficient, you drink more water, and you breathe in fewer pollutants. A whole range of health factors improve simply by living at higher elevations.[8]

At Snowridge, every day was active. We spent all day on our feet, hiking, building, cleaning, and playing. When we weren't on our feet, we were in a white water rafting tube. We all lost weight that summer, despite a steady diet of camp food and our weekly camp challenge to consume an entire bottle of honey in one sitting without, well...you know.

Central to our enjoyment of God's creation is the physical capacity to enjoy that creation.

Now, before I get too far into this section, let me pause to address the obvious elephant in the room. Many children have limited mobility for one reason or another. Does this mean they are relegated to second-tier status when it comes to enjoying life? Not in the slightest. All of us will encounter limitations when it comes to our physical abilities.

Even with great challenges, there is beauty, goodness, and joy to be found in the disciplined use of our bodies. I think of Joni Eareckson Tada, who, while unable to use her hands, is able to paint by holding a brush in her mouth. I

---

7. Cal Newport, *Digital Minimalism* (Penguin LLC, 2019), 130.
8. Martin Burtscher, "Effects of Living at Higher Altitudes on Mortality: A Narrative Review," *Aging and Disease* 5, no. 4 (2014): 274–80, https://www.ncbi.nlm.nih.gov/pmc/articles/PMC4113517/.

think of Bethany Hamilton, the professional surfer who lost an arm at the age of thirteen to a shark attack and still went on to have an impressive career riding the biggest waves in the world. While both of these women are outliers in every sense of the word, there are everyday, ordinary ways we can enjoy the bodies God has given us no matter how limited we may be.

The foundation of our desire for physical fitness must lie in its important role in our spiritual and holistic health and joy. David Mathis has even referred to fitness as a spiritual discipline, in that it sees us as embodied creatures—those made by God with good bodies that are made for good things.[9]

Prior to the proliferation of the internet in the 1990s, regular human movement was assumed. However, nearly every technological improvement throughout time has only made us more sedentary. Our ancestors had to grow and/or kill any food they ate. Then came markets where we could barter with food suppliers, and then grocery stores, grocery delivery, and now home-delivery meal kits. Gathering food was not always a net calorie-positive activity. Now we just have to expend whatever energy it takes to tap some buttons, breathe, and blink our eyes. I, like some of you, work from home. My office is twenty steps from my bedroom. There are many days I am certain my total step count is only in the hundreds. Much like our children's bodies, my body, too, has kept the score of this denial of humanity in the form of emotional dysregulation, weight gain, and the fact that I can't do an afternoon of yard work without feeling the need to be carried off on a stretcher.

The Bible encourages us to think better about our physicality. While the Bible is not a book about physical fitness, it does have a great deal to say about the value of the body.

Psalm 139:13-14 says,

---

9. David Mathis, "A Little Theology of Exercise," Inspire 2000 Conference, desiringGod, March 22, 2020, https://www.desiringgod.org/messages/a-little-theology-of-exercise.

> You formed my inward parts;
> you knitted me together in my mother's womb.
> I praise you, for I am fearfully and wonderfully made.

This psalm is much more than a pro-life text. It is a pro-body text. The psalmist marvels at how each part of his body is precisely engineered to work together to praise God. He made our feet to run through trails in the woods and our cheeks to feel the cool breeze. He designed our hands to build, make, shape, and create. Our eyes were specifically engineered to be a lamp to our whole body, filling us with the light of the glory of God (Matthew 6:22).

Not only did God make our bodies with tremendous intent, they also belong to him. Paul writes in 1 Corinthians 6:19-20, "Do you not know that your body is a temple of the Holy Spirit within you, whom you have from God? You are not your own, for you were bought with a price."

This verse stands in stark opposition to any notion that the body is of little importance. It is simply unbiblical to believe our bodies are merely transport vessels from one life into the next or that they are to be used and abused in any way we see fit. Instead, they are the dwelling place of the Holy Spirit. They were purchased by Jesus for his glory and our enjoyment.

Paul writes later in 1 Corinthians 10:31, "Whether you eat or drink, or whatever you do, do all to the glory of God." In a nutshell, this verse says, "God made you, and so his imprint is all over everything you do. What you do with your bodies matters. It brings him glory or is something done in vain."

Again, David Mathis is helpful here: "God plainly commends the exertion of our bodies through the effort of work (Ephesians 4:28; 2 Thessalonians 3:10), even hard work (2 Timothy 2:6)—that we not be idle, but 'busy at work' (2 Thessalonians 3:11). Laziness is sin, and a physical and spiritual danger (Proverbs 21:25)."[10]

---

10. Mathis, "A Little Theology of Exercise."

The Bible is clear on these things: (1) God made our bodies. (2) God calls us to steward our bodies. (3) God calls us to enjoy our bodies. (4) God calls us to use our bodies. All four of these truths are unto the end that we would glorify God with our bodies.

While we may disagree with Plato on the specifics of this claim, we can affirm the merits: "In order for man to succeed in life, God provided him with two means, education and physical activity. Not separately, one for the soul and the other for the body, but for the two together. With these two means, man can attain perfection."[11]

So parents, it is your job to fight the tough, uphill battle of getting your kids back outside. If your children have fallen into the habit of having multiple hours of screen time each day, this will not be easy. Their brains have literally been rewired to require their devices for the dopamine their brains need to function properly. They may be addicts, and the earlier you realize that getting your kids back outside to play is not too dissimilar from sending an alcoholic to rehab, the more successful you will be in the long run. This is not to be crass or insensitive to the pain of substance abuse but simply to recognize the seriousness of what we're dealing with.

The kicker—if your kids are addicted to screens, you likely are too. It's a learned behavior. Take stock of your resistance and possibly even your failed previous attempts to help your children break the cycle. How much of it was your unwillingness to change your own habits?

The great news is that you are not alone in this good work. Others have gone before you, and still more will follow. Two traveling companions I heartily recommend are Molly DeFrank (*Digital Detox*) and Ginny Yurich (*1000 Hours Outside*). They are not superheroes. They are parents like you and me who have

---

11. Gotama Akṣapāda, *PLATO'S DOCTRINE: 909 Relics of Greek Philosophy* (Independently Published, 2019).

had to navigate the complexities and challenges of our modern age and have had some success doing so.

Remember as we close this section…you have the freedom to try and fail. Discipling your children to care well for their bodies, like anything else, will come with its share of difficulties. Maintain a posture of kindness toward yourself and your family. Negativity will only breed failure.

Finally, feel the freedom to release your children to God. They are already his, after all. You did not knit together their inward parts (Psalm 139:13). God did. Put your children in the places God has promised to work—using their bodies for the glory of God. Then get out of the way and watch as they wonder at the amazing ways God has created all things, including them!

Discipling with the End in Mind

There is, of course, a much larger purpose for discipling our children in the enjoyment and care of their bodies. Isaiah 40:31 paints a picture of our future glorified bodies:

> But they who wait for the LORD shall renew their strength;
> they shall mount up with wings like eagles;
> they shall run and not be weary;
> they shall walk and not faint.

Even the reminders of our limited physical abilities, our stymied attempts at creativity, and our clumsy ventures into play remind us that a day is coming where we will play, create, and move our bodies with no strain or limitations.

Our children can play a game of soccer and imagine a day where they will be able to play forever without getting tired, sore, injured, or frustrated. Even the enjoyment they get from playing with friends on this side of eternity is but a minute glimmer of the future that awaits them.

CHAPTER 8

Discipling the Mind

I never set out to work with children. In fact, it was one of the last things I wanted to do after growing up as the son of an elementary school teacher. I went to college to be a doctor, but that plan was foiled because of a trigonometry professor and a deficient mathematics department at the major university I attended. Because I was premed, trigonometry was mandatory (because the Pythagorean theorem apparently is clutch in the surgical arena). Unfortunately, the only professor who taught trigonometry had perhaps the strongest accent and the least patience of any human I've ever known.

Countless times I went to his office hours, and even there I could only understand every fifth word he spoke. It was well known among students that you basically had to teach yourself, grin and bear it, and just get through it. It was miserable; I did my best and got a D. I dropped out of premed and eventually wound up as an elementary education major because it was the easiest major I could find, and after running the gauntlet of trigonometry, I felt I deserved a break.[1]

I'm an intelligent person. I'm sure that if I took the same class with a professor who possessed a better command of the English language and a face that didn't look at me like I was an idiot every time I asked a question, I would have managed to squeak out the required B- to remain on the premed track.

What happened to me is not all too dissimilar from many children's experiences of discipleship, both in the home and in the church. Adults can have a hard time remembering what it was like to be a child. We find it challenging to speak in ways they'll understand.

Just this past Sunday, I watched as one of my well-intentioned Sunday school teachers attempted to explain and apply the laws of supply and demand in a lesson for a group of pre-K students. My four-year-old was in the class, and the best part of my day was watching her do this thing where she cranes her neck to the side and squints an eye when she doesn't have a clue what you're talking about. Adorable.

A Crisis of Priority

The cognitive gap between the adult brain and the child brain is one of the most undervalued challenges not only in the church but also in life. It is for this reason that we must place a high bar for the care of our children. Sadly, though, this is a challenge the church consistently underestimates.

---

1. Speaking of breaks…I just took a break from writing to see if he's still teaching. HE IS! Twenty-two years later, the same class! After a therapeutic deep dive on ratemyprofessors.com, I've now confirmed that my story is not unique.

Every week, I speak with churches whose spoken or unspoken ethos is to place ministry to children at the bottom of the staffing and serving priority list.

Just recently, I heard one leader remark that their children's ministry would be a great place for new church members to "get their feet wet." I spoke to another on the phone, looking to hire a full-time children's pastor for less than someone could make working full time at Ace Hardware. (No shade on Ace—you truly are the place with the helpful hardware folks!) An experienced elder in our church once suggested we hire a young female right out of college as our children's director because we could "pay her less." Recently, I spoke at a small children's ministry conference and asked as many people as I could, "What did you study in college?" Maybe 10 percent studied something in the field of elementary education, Christian education, or child development.

This is a tragedy. I'll just call it what it is—pastoral malpractice, and it harms our children in at least four ways:

1. **We put our most vulnerable people (children) with our least qualified adults.** This is unfortunate both from an instructional and a safety perspective.

2. **We understate the enormously difficult task of teaching children.** It is much, much easier to teach adults. Every time I finish teaching a room of adults, I leave thinking, *Golly, that was easy*. This is not a brag, but after two decades in children's ministry, I feel like I am just now getting to the point that I can open my Bible and start teaching children with very little preparation.

3. **We cheapen the work of discipling children.** If a parent sees a church placing discipleship as a low value, how can we possibly expect families to place it as a high value?

4. **Our children are watching.** My eleven-year-old notices what our church prioritizes. He sees what gets airtime during announcements. He sees where the best staff and volunteers are. If our children get the short end of the stick, we give them a steep hill to climb to see their value.

When parents and churches do not mind the gap between the adult brain and the child brain, we have a recipe for disaster. That disaster has the name *impatience*. When we subconsciously expect children to reason like adults, we become quick-tempered with the most impressionable people in our lives. The Bible has some counsel for us to grow in our patience with our children.

Galatians 6:2 encourages us to "bear one another's burdens, and so fulfill the law of Christ." Which law? The law of loving our neighbors. When we carry burdens others cannot carry for themselves, we care well for them. To carry someone's burden, you must understand them, know them, study them, see them—really, really *see* them. One of the unique burdens of childhood is that children are not ready physically, socially, emotionally, or spiritually for nearly everything they encounter. Almost every word, place, and concept is a first-time experience.

When adults understand and allow this truth to shape their practice, our children experience it as a tremendous display of love. We bear our children's burdens when we see them, know them, and then prepare to live life alongside them in a way that honors childhood as a gift and not a liability.

Seeing our children as those growing in their knowledge, skills, and abilities helps them feel safe. When we feel safe, we can experience love. When we feel both safe and loved, we can grow, learn, and become the people we were meant to be.

Similarly, Romans 12:18 encourages us, "If it is possible, as far as it depends on you, live at peace with everyone" (NIV). Understanding child development steadies us as parents. It moderates our disappointments and expectations. I've never met a parent who went into the business of parenting to have a terrible time, and yet so many do. Knowing our children's limitations and potential helps us extend patience, gentleness, and kindness. It helps us live at peace where we would otherwise become demanding, harsh, and impatient.

This week I have to put together four pieces of IKEA furniture. I would never dream of putting even these simple pieces together without an owner's manual. And yet most parents think they can raise children without reading the manual and learning how their brains and bodies work. The more I am around children and parents, I think an enormous portion of parental frustration can be mitigated simply by understanding how children develop.[2]

Christian parents would do well to have a Bible in one hand and at least a rudimentary understanding of child development in the other. There is a surprising amount of disagreement about this in Christian circles. Some claim that inserting child development knowledge into discipleship would "dumb down" the process and "not allow the Spirit to work." Others object to thinking of child development alongside discipleship because we shouldn't need any more than what the Bible provides to understand children. Including psychology and secular thought in discipleship seems, to some, unnecessary and perhaps even harmful.

I understand the heart behind these arguments, but I think they are largely based on unsubstantiated fears. God has provided us with common grace to help

---

2. Obviously, there is no comprehensive owner's manual for how to raise each unque child! However, there are people God has chosen to work through by his common grace who can help us better understand the intricacies of child development.

us navigate life in a challenging world. This includes professionals who devote their lives to studying children. Even Jesus understood the profound difference between adults and children. Notice how he spoke to children differently than he spoke to adults. And so I would like to offer the following counsel when it comes to pairing a knowledge of child development with discipleship. Bearing the burdens of childhood takes work, but it is not impossible. All it requires is a lot of prayer and a little trip back to your freshman-year psychology class. Each of the theories below has its strengths and weaknesses. None fully explains the complexity of the developing mind. However, each one gives us a window into loving our closest neighbors—our children—well. Let's start with the basics.

Children Are Social Learners

Lev Vygotsky's work is foundational to what has become known as *sociocultural theory*. Believing that cognitive development is directly influenced by cultural and social factors, Vygotsky was one of the first researchers to believe that our communities play integral roles in the process of *making meaning*.

In his view, our cognitive development is directly related to our socialization with friends, family members, and teachers. We gain greater and greater levels of understanding as we learn from "more knowledgeable others." For the sake of simplicity, we will simply refer to "more knowledgeable others" as "mentors." These mentors are teachers, parents, coaches, pastors, and even peers who help guide children into deeper understanding of everything from mathematics to language to, yes, knowledge of God.

In terms Jesus may have used, we grow in our knowledge when we are covered in the dust of more knowledgeable others. According to Vygotsky, we achieve optimal development in supportive communities where we grow alongside those who've gone before us.

One of the most enduring tools of Vygotsky's work is that of *scaffolding*. In simple terms, children can learn more when mentors provide support to help children learn skills just beyond their current level. Through collaborative dialogue, children seek to understand what the mentor knows and internalize that new information into their own knowledge base.

Mentors, in Vygotsky's view, serve as guides who help us move from basic to more complex levels of understanding over time. In a sense, mentors build bridges between what we know today and what we are capable of knowing tomorrow. Vygotsky referred to this as the zone of proximal development, which you might think of as a child's stretch goal. This important concept relates to the difference between what a child can achieve independently and what a child can achieve with guidance and encouragement from a mentor.

Because of this, Vygotsky focused closely on social interaction as an aid to learning, arguing that when left alone, children will develop—but not to their full potential.

Vygotsky is a fascinating conversation partner when it comes to discipleship. So much of what he teaches is reflected in the Bible's value of shared community. His theory provides many helpful paradigms for discipleship, including these important foundations:

1. Children need the guidance of adults and older children.

Discipleship is a social endeavor. In a world of online school, virtual church, and remote learning, the task of discipleship cannot be outsourced. It is best done in physical community with others.

2. Discipling children in their knowledge of God is an iterative process.

Parents can help children build on previous knowledge of God gradually and through collaborative dialogue. Guiding our children through stretch goals involves knowing what they know and then guiding them to deeper understanding. For instance, a three-year-old may understand that God made them in a general sense. The next step may be to talk about the particulars of why God made them: to glorify him, to enjoy his creation, to love one another, and so on.

Children Are Needy Learners

Maslow may be one of the most well loved of all the social psychologists. His hierarchy of needs is likely the one thing you remember from psychology class. But what, exactly, is a book on discipleship doing talking about a theory that has self-fulfillment at the apex of the human experience? Bear with me. Maslow's terminology may not be as helpful on the surface, but the common grace of God is still all over his work.

You may remember seeing Maslow's famous pyramid. It comprises five levels of human needs. A person must have their needs met at one level of the pyramid before they can move up to the next level.

At the bottom of the pyramid are two needs: physiological and safety. Physiological needs refer to the most primitive needs of children: food, water, warmth, rest, shelter, and clothing. If children do not possess these, they cannot move to the next level: safety. Safety is the need for children to feel order, predictability, and control in their lives. Children who have their safety needs met feel socially stable, medically well, and relatively free from fear.

The next two levels of the pyramid are belongingness needs and esteem needs. Belongingness needs refer to children's need for relationships, connectedness, and the feeling of being part of a group. This need is particularly important to children, so much so that teens will often prioritize belonging over safety and, in the worst of cases, even their physiological needs. The need to feel needed is powerful. The next level up once belongingness needs are met is that of esteem needs. This includes feelings of self-worth, respect, and value.

The highest level on the hierarchy is self-actualization, which refers to children who are able to realize their full potential and seek personal growth.

Now, how did Maslow find its way into a book on discipleship? The answer lies in the fact that this theory helps us see children as humans living actual lives in a broken, fallen world. Many parents demand obedience when their kids just need a snack, expect lonely children to fulfill their potential, and want kids who need naps to respect one another.

Please don't hear what I'm not saying. Children should learn to obey when they're hungry. They need to grow in respecting one another when they are tired. However, these skills take time to develop. Maslow adds detail to our conversation on discipleship in the following ways:

1. Our children are people with needs that need to be valued.

Their needs for sleep and safety are not optional side dishes. They are the main course, the foundation of stability from which children can grow. These basic needs are God-given gifts that speak to our limited humanity and our need to honor our bodies.

2. Our children need to find their people.

In an age of growing isolation among children, parents need to help cultivate friendships among peers. To be sure, this may require you breaking the social isolation you may have set for yourself! Relationships are not "nice to have," but are essential for our growth.

3. Our children trust and learn from adults who honor their personhood.

When your child is having a hard time not giving you a hard time, take a few steps back and see the context of the situation. Are they cold and need a jacket? Do they feel left out of an activity? Reflective parents who know their children's core needs become safe places for children to grow.

The Different Stages of Child Development

Nobody has been more helpful to me in teaching children than the work of Jean Piaget. His four simple categories help me understand where a child is in their cognitive development. Developmental maturity has enormous implications for what children are capable of learning and how they reason. Importantly, for growing disciples, our capacity to comprehend the work of God grows as our minds grow.

Below, I've provided brief descriptions of each stage and some practical insights. Although I've listed ages for each stage, know that children move through stages at their own unique pace and these should be treated only as guidelines.

Stage 1: Sensorimotor (Birth to two years)

The first stage is the sensorimotor stage, during which infants focus on physical sensations and learning to coordinate their bodies. During the sensorimotor stage, a range of cognitive abilities develop. These include object permanence (objects can disappear from sight and still exist), self-recognition (the child realizes that other people are separate from them), deferred imitation (they can replicate an action sometime after they first see someone else do it), and representational play. During this stage, children begin to gain a capacity known as *general symbolic function*, which is the ability to imagine something when it is not physically present.

During the beginning of this stage, infants live in the present. They do not have a mental picture of the world stored in their memory. If they cannot see something, then it does not exist.

This is why you can hide a toy from an infant while they watch, but they will not search for the object once it has left their sight.

The main achievement during this stage is object permanence—knowing that an object still exists, even if it is hidden. It requires the ability to form a mental representation of the object.

By this point you may be thinking, "What does this have to do with discipleship?" Answer: a lot. From the time children are born, they engage in a rapid process of learning about the world God made. Everything they encounter is new, full of possibilities, and marvelous. Parents often remark that their children are more interested in empty paper towel rolls than their carefully curated, aesthetically pleasing, neutral colored, allergen-free, seventy-five dollar wooden blocks from Pottery Barn.[3] This phenomenon exists because the paper towel roll is just as novel to them as the blocks. Here are a few takeaways from this stage:

1. **Enjoy this stage.** You don't get it back. Parenting is physically exhausting in these early years, but your child will never learn at such a rapid rate ever again in their entire lives.

2. **Don't sweat the small stuff in this stage.** Many parents have asked me what they can do to disciple their infants. There's always a hint of anxiety in their voices, as if they may have missed out on something important, dooming their child to a life of playing catch-up. What your children need most in this stage are not memory verses or catechisms. They need you. They need to feel the undeserved, steady guiding hand of their parents. Later, this will help them recognize and trust these characteristics in God.

---

3. It's true. I just looked it up. And it was on sale.

3. **Surround your children with the beauty of God's creation.**
   Spend time outdoors. Resist the urge to put kids in front of
   screens (even though it is completely fine if you need five
   minutes to shower, or cry, or both). Let them touch, smell,
   taste, and listen to as many things as possible. Their brains
   build connections at lightning speed in this stage. Loving
   parents know this and let their infants begin to be covered
   in the dust of Jesus by interacting with all the wonderful
   things he has made.

4. **Your child's lack of object permanence means the concept
   of a God who exists but cannot be seen is incredibly
   challenging.** This does not mean, however, that children
   cannot begin to associate God and the things of God (the
   church, Christians, and virtues) with goodness, truth, and
   beauty.

Stage 2: Preoperational (Ages two to seven years)

At the beginning of this stage, children's thinking is influenced
by the way things appear rather than logical reasoning. Further-
more, children are egocentric at this stage; they assume that
other people see the world as they do.

As the preoperational stage progresses, egocentrism declines,
and children begin to enjoy including other children in their
games. During this time, "imaginary play" becomes more important. Toddlers often pretend to be people they are not (for
example, superheroes or policemen) and may play these roles
with props that symbolize real-life objects. Children may also
invent an imaginary playmate. This imaginary play is key to children maturing out of egocentrism and into becoming people of
empathy, understanding, and compassion.

During this stage, young children can think about things symbolically, which is the ability to make one thing, such as a word or an object, stand for something other than itself. For example, a child in this stage will come to associate the symbol of a stop sign with the physical action of stopping and looking both ways, even if they can't read the word *stop*.

Though symbolic thinking develops at this age, their logical thinking usually develops later. A preoperational child's thinking is still dominated by how the world looks, not how the world is. You might insist they need to bring a rain jacket to school because the weather man said it's going to rain later this afternoon. However, if it is bright and sunny out in the morning when they leave, the rain jacket makes no sense to them.

Children also struggle with nuance in this stage. Practically, this means children may be able to sort ideas into general categories but have a more difficult time sorting things into subcategories. This can create black-and-white thinking among children in the preoperational stage.

Here are a few takeaways from this stage:

1. **This is the trickiest stage for most parents.** Children seem to be capable of so much during this stage, and yet they still have a long way to go. Be patient. Your child can do so much more at the end of this stage than at the beginning, and yet they still have so far to go.

2. **This stage is when parents and church leaders usually begin teaching the Bible in a more systematic way.** This is a good and right impulse. Kids in this stage are sponges. To not teach the Bible during this stage is a missed

opportunity. That being said, know that children will struggle with the following:

- The ability to put themselves in someone else's shoes. Their egocentrism has a hard time thinking about how anyone else feels but them. This is not a deficiency; it's simply something that must develop over time. Children may have a hard time identifying with the experiences of those in the Bible or thinking about things from God's perspective instead of their own.

- Logical thought, which may ask a child to think, *If A and B are true, then what might be true of C?* Unfortunately for children at this stage, this is classic biblical application. Children will have trouble in this stage extrapolating the stories and truths they learn about in God's word to their experience of everyday life.

- Nuanced thought, such as the ability to think in shades of gray rather than black and white. For instance, the sinner-saint paradigm is a stretch at this stage. It is also difficult for children to understand how Jesus can be simultaneously God and man or how he can be both omnipotent and suffer death on a cross. Paradigms that present dilemmas will almost always stump children in this stage.

3. **A key capacity of this stage is that of symbolism.** Children can attach memories to images, songs, numbers, smells, and any number of things. When teaching the Bible to children in the preoperational stage, props, manipulatives, pictures, and music are essential for good teaching. One of my favorite lessons each year is one where I burn frankincense in a room full of preoperational kids as I teach the story of the wise men's visit in Luke 2. No child ever forgets that story because the smell is so memorable.

Stage 3: Concrete Operational (Ages seven to eleven)

The beginning of this stage is marked by the onset of logical thinking and the ability to see the world through the eyes of others. These strides are monumental, but children in this stage still experience difficulty with abstract thinking.

During this stage, children understand the concept of conservation—that although things may change, certain properties can remain the same. A classic example of conservation is the ability to know that while a tall, skinny glass of water may appear to have more water because of its height, the same quantity of water can also exist in a short, squatty glass.

Children in this stage also develop the ability to think in reverse (which comes in handy when they lose their shoes for the umpteenth time).

Piaget considered the concrete stage a major turning point in children's cognitive development because it marks the beginning of operational thought. This means children can process situations internally in their head (rather than physically in the real world). Simply put, they can imagine the consequences of their actions prior to engaging in the action. Similarly, they can paint mental pictures of events that are described to them without needing to see the events first.

Here are a few takeaways from this stage:

1. **Children in the concrete operational stage gain a great deal from reflecting on ideas with others and individually.** Providing children the opportunity to talk with peers and adults about concepts is key during this stage. Creating times where children can journal and write ideas helps encourage their development of logical thinking.

2. **Because of the developing skill of conservation, they can more readily understand the never-changing character of God.** Jesus is the same when he is with the Father and the Spirit in creation and in his life, death, resurrection, and ascension. His nature is unchangeable even through physical changes. Similarly, children learn one of the greatest comforts any of us can know—that God is the same in his actions and affections despite our fluctuating obedience and faithfulness.

3. **Many children, especially those raised in the church, will profess faith in this stage.** To be clear, salvation is always a work of the Spirit and is always a miracle whenever it happens. However, children in this stage can more readily understand the logic between their sinfulness and their need for a Savior. I happen to think it's no mistake that children in this stage also get their first megadoses of "real life problems." As they are rightfully given more independence and freedom, friends may betray them and their mistakes have real consequences. For Jesus to meet children in this stage is a real sign of his kindness.

Stage 4: Formal Operational (Ages twelve and over)

The formal operational stage begins around age twelve. As children enter this stage, they gain the abilities to think in an abstract manner, to combine and classify items in a more sophisticated way, and to reason at a higher order. Adolescents can think systematically about what might be as well as what is.

It is important to note that not everyone will reach this stage, even into adulthood. The capacity to engage in thought that allows us to hold multiple viewpoints and theories in tension is not achieved by everyone.

Most teenagers, however, can deal with abstract ideas. They can solve problems in their minds and imagine hypothetical situations. Teenagers can speculate and draw conclusions that those at younger ages are unable to.

Here are a few takeaways from this stage:

1. **Once teenagers grow into abstract thinking, their learning and development skyrocket.** They can handle a tremendous amount of challenges in this stage that they were incapable of in previous stages. Encourage daily prayer and Bible study in this stage. The temptation of this stage is to become overly reliant on their ability to figure things out on their own. What a gift to engage the challenges of everyday life with the word of God. Lifelong habits of trust and dependence on God can be established in this stage.

2. **Engage in deep conversations with teenagers—perhaps even deeper than you thought possible.** They are curious and are drawing conclusions about the world around them at a rapid rate. They need the guidance of their parents as they grow in reason about God's world.

3. **Teenagers can live in biblical tensions that younger children could not understand because they lacked the ability to think hypothetically and abstractly.** The tension of God's justice and love, the wonder of the "already and not yet," and the dilemma of simultaneously being sinful and yet a saint will stimulate teenagers to think deeply about the nature of God and their place in his kingdom.

Closing Thoughts

Admittedly, this is a bit out of context, but Paul comments in 1 Corinthians 13:11, "When I was a child, I spoke like a child, I thought like a child, I reasoned like a child. When I became a man, I gave up childish ways." What is true about this verse is that it comes in the context of 1 Corinthians' famous passage on love:

> Love is patient and kind; love does not envy or boast; it is not arrogant or rude. It does not insist on its own way; it is not irritable or resentful; it does not rejoice at wrongdoing, but rejoices with the truth. Love bears all things, believes all things, hopes all things, endures all things (1 Corinthians 13:4-7).

We love our children well when we understand the massive difference between a child and an adult. While our children are children, they will speak, think, and reason as children. As they grow, they will change. Parents, love your children well by knowing the ways they develop. In the end, it will help you be patient, kind, not envious or boastful, not arrogant or rude, not insistent on your own way, and…at least a little less irritable.

CHAPTER 9

Discipling the Emotions, Part 1: Our Emotional Roots

As a child, I received little in the way of training in emotional awareness. If anything, I intuited that my feelings, especially the so-called negative ones, were a hindrance to the adults around me. As I've worked with thousands of children, I know that "little Chris" is not alone. On a weekly basis, I see kids who have learned to…

…moderate their hopes and dreams.

…hide and numb their pain.

…shame themselves for feeling the way they do.

…deny their needs to placate others.

These coping mechanisms are, at their root, failures to live fully. If you'll remember, back in Genesis 1–3, God called the first couple to enjoy the garden, to marvel at all God had revealed to them. Instead, Adam and Eve traded honesty for hiding. They went into a fight-or-flight survival mode, which was far, far from their intended purpose to live honestly and truthfully and bear the image of God, who is always honest and truthful.

Our children were born into this reality. Their hearts are hungry to live fully, and yet both personal and corporate sinfulness prevent them from doing so. The solution to this dilemma is twofold.

First, our children (and their parents) must come to terms with the knowledge that things will only be so good on this side of heaven. Even though we long for a life without pain, it's simply part of the human experience. The paradox of living fully in the midst of pain is to see things like fear and sadness as gifts (more on this in the next chapter).

Second, our children need relationships. Relationships are not simply the cherry on top once we have all our other needs met. They are the central need of humanity. The Trinity itself is the Godhead living in relationship with one another. Being an image-bearer is living in the reality that God told Adam, *before the fall*, that it was not good for him to be alone. Our children's need for nurturing friends, loving parents, and supportive mentors is not a result of sin. It is simply a part of being created by God. Even in the womb, relationships occur. Unborn children respond to their parent's voices with increased heart rates and movement. As soon as babies are born, they are soothed by their mother's touch. We do not outgrow this need for relationships. Parents do well to nurture relational desire in their children, as it will carry them through the challenging years of their youth into adulthood.

Emotionally Mature Parents

While some genetic factors cause children to struggle with their feelings, more times than not, emotionally immature children come from the homes of emotionally immature parents. In these settings, children lack the safety needed to grow into fullhearted adults who are capable of trusting God amid the struggles and triumphs of life, blessing their families and friends, and enjoying the lives God invites them to inhabit.

Emotionally mature and immature parents come in all shapes and sizes. Some are easy to spot, and some hide in plain sight. Perhaps it is best to compare the two with a few examples:

Emotionally immature parents...	Emotionally mature parents...
...are dependent on their children for their emotional well-being.	...have a well-defined sense of self. They know where they end and their children begin.
...rely on comparison and critique to center their sense of self-worth.	...celebrate differences among peers and appreciate the unique contributions of various thoughts, feelings, and opinions.
...do not take appropriate responsibility when they are wrong.	...accept proper responsibility and repair damaged relationships.

Recognizing the specks of immaturity in yourself can be one of the greatest gifts you will ever give your children. Admitting that you have room to grow is not a weakness. It is human. Those willing to gain humility through knowledge of their own weaknesses become safer people to be around. In a sense, they emulate what is commended in Titus 2:2-3: "Older men are to be sober-minded, dignified, self-controlled, sound in faith, in love, and in steadfastness. Older women likewise are to be reverent in behavior, not slanderers or slaves to much wine."

Sober-minded people are reflective and careful.

Those who are reverent in behavior act in ways that show deference to others.

The Bible continually celebrates older men and women—parents, we might say—who perpetually think of the needs of others, are suspicious of their own claims to goodness, and honor everyone they come into contact with, no matter their age.

These sober-minded parents often raise emotionally mature children not because they have some special character-forming curriculum. These parents are not perfect. In fact, they may "mess up" more than unsafe parents. But what they do for their children is profound. They are safe people who reflect the character of Christ in their homes.

Safe parents are simply those with softened hearts, who are learning to apply the gospel to their lives. Safe parents know that they are but merely children of God themselves, and the Spirit continually testifies to this fact.[1] Safe parents do not depend on others for their emotional well-being. Instead, they have a sense of self defined by God. Safe parents do not build their self-esteem on the backs of the perceived mistakes of others; they honor everyone, regardless of their station in life. Safe parents do not compile lists of examples to defend their righteousness in the midst of failure; instead, they repair relationships by accepting responsibility and building trust.

At the core of discipling children in their emotions is the creation of this type of safety. Here's why...

A lack of safety, at its root, is a lack of feeling loved. Contrary to what we might think, the opposite of love is not hate. It's fear.[2] The apostle John says, "There is no fear in love. But perfect love drives out fear, because fear has to do with punishment. The one who fears is not made perfect in love" (1 John 4:18 NIV). Children who grow up in fearful environments may learn to survive, but

---

1. Romans 8:16.
2. Joshua Straub, *Safe House*, 20.

they may never learn to thrive. They feel sad, glad, and mad but lack the skills necessary to allow those emotions to lead them to places of health.

This reality is a big part of my story. "Little Chris" learned to survive, and it's led to a tremendous amount of pain in my adult life. Perhaps like you, I am uncovering my emotional world as an adult and am finding healing, which is why I am passionate about helping parents embrace the privilege of discipling their children in emotional health.

Discipling our children in emotional health is an opportunity to change the world. Adults wreck their lives every day, not because they lack knowledge but because they lack the emotional intelligence to navigate life in a fallen world. Emotional health is far from a nice add-on to a good life. Instead, it is the very pathway through which we love the Lord with all our heart, mind, and strength and love our neighbors as we love ourselves.

Our Emotional Roots

The most helpful resource I've found both personally and in my ministry to families is that of the Spiritual Root System from Sage Hill Ministries.[3] I owe a great deal to them for what proceeds in the rest of this chapter and the next. What follows is an adapted version of their system with children in mind.[4]

The controlling metaphor of the system is a picture of the heart as a tree. Just as a tree must absorb water and nutrients for survival, so the heart has roots that must access the necessities of life: feelings, needs, desires, longings, and hopes. These roots are not an unfortunate by-product of being human. They are not a burden. In fact, they are the way God designed us to interact with his world. Parents do well to encourage the growth of these roots in their children.

---

3. "The Spiritual Root System," Sage Hill, January 1, 2019, https://www.sagehill.co/blog/spiritual-root-system.
4. Admittedly, what follows in this chapter and the next is not a one-size-fits-all approach. Many people of all ages and stages face unique circumstances and challenges, but these principles can be a helpful jumping-off point.

Feelings

I imagined the birth of our first son as a beautiful scene where he would peacefully enter the arms of his parents. As you may know, childbirth is anything but that. From the moment my son was born, he was at war with the world. He was a screaming, slightly blue, angry ball of feelings.

Feelings are primal. They are subconscious. We use feelings to communicate our needs. To live fully, our children need to gain the skills to communicate their feelings with clarity and honesty. In fact, feelings are the foundational root. All the other roots find their foundations in our feelings. For that reason, in the next chapter, we'll look more specifically at how to help our children identify, own, and grow through their feelings.

Needs

When we learn to deny our feelings, we begin to survive. When we survive, we deny our needs. God created us to need more than the basics. In fact, the more mature we are, the more needy we may become. Needs are not signs of weakness. Instead, they are honest expressions of our vulnerability and desire to be cared for. For example, we have needs for security, touch, safety, belonging, grief, trust, support, attention, guidance, and significance.

Take, for instance, the need for guidance. Our children need a significant amount of guidance as they grow—on everything from how to tie their shoes to how to navigate bullies. However, many of us believe their need for guidance diminishes as they age. The vulnerabilities they experienced as children become masked by the Western values of self-sufficiency and independence. Over time, these children grow into adults who look around to find they have lost much of the guidance they need.

While we once needed our parents for more primitive requirements, adulthood brings about a new set of even more complex challenges. A denial of our need for guidance leads to anxiety and loneliness in adulthood. Parents who have denied their needs tend to raise children who deny their needs as well. After all, if dad never needs to ask for help and seems annoyed when I ask for help, then maybe the way to life is to not be so needy.

Helping our children embrace their needs as a necessary, not unfortunate, component of living life fully will produce fruitful children who grow into mature adulthood and trust God to provide through the people he brings to our lives.

Desires

When we communicate our hunger for something bigger than ourselves, we reveal our desires. Communicating desire is a courageous act of vulnerability, as it shows how much we want something. Desires are powerful motivators. We will go through tremendous amounts of emotional, physical, and spiritual pain to pursue them.

Our children need supportive spaces where they can communicate their desires to peers and adults who will remain receptive and non-judgmental. Children who grow up without this support do not lose their desires; they simply pursue their desires in unhealthy ways. What was once a pure desire, gifted to them by God, becomes a bizarre expression of corruption:

Their desire for beauty and love becomes a lust for sex.

Their desire for truth becomes a need for control.

Their desire for justice becomes a demanding nature.

Their desire for success becomes a pursuit of fame.

When we listen to, celebrate, and give shape to our children's desires, we help remove their hesitations to pursue them in healthy ways. By lending a safe, understanding, and curious ear to our children's desires, we may find that they find the relational space to chase their desires in healthy ways:

Their desire for beauty and love becomes a pursuit of friendship.

Their desire for truth becomes a quest for holiness.

Their desire for justice becomes a winsome posture of mercy, kindness, and grace.

Their desire for success becomes a humble aspiration of excellence for God's glory and the service of others.

Longings

Closely related to desires, but more primitive, are longings for justice, rest, peace, safety, and home. These longings are the expression of the image of God in our children and in us. Even more than that, these longings point to a time when our longings will be fully satisfied.

For example, our children wrestle with the injustice of how some people's bodies and minds work in different, sometimes better ways. Some of our children excel in school, and some will find learning to be an uphill battle. Some of our children experience physical limitations, while others have seemingly boundless energy and abilities. Parents have options:

One is to encourage our children to put their longings on a pedestal as motivation to try harder, be better, and do more. Certainly, we should support our children in pursuit of becoming all that God has made them to be. However, we should never manipulate their honest expressions of pain by turning them into moralistic motivational messages. This will only produce shame and the coping mechanism of hiding their longings and not experiencing the freedom of the gospel.

A second option is to help children see their longings as good reminders of eternity. Their longings bear witness to the perfection we are wired for. Some of our longings may be met on this side of heaven. Some of them may only be met when we see Jesus face-to-face. Parents who engage their children's longings on this level push back the curtain of shame that often clouds our unmet longings and open their child's heart to the limitation of this life and the wonder of the life to come.

Hopes

Babies are full of hope. They reach out for their parents and expect a response. They cry and know someone will come to comfort them. Nearly everything they do expresses the belief that someone will meet their needs.

The writer of Proverbs was on to something when he wrote, "Hope deferred makes the heart sick, but a longing fulfilled is a tree of life" (Proverbs 13:12 NIV). When we find others who meet us in our hopes, faith grows. When someone sees our hopes and honors them, we have something tangible for what was previously unseen.

We wound children when we minimize and diminish their hopes. Parents serve their children well when they take their hopes seriously by listening and then providing avenues for their hopes to be realized in reasonable ways.

Remember these five roots: feelings, needs, desires, longings, and hopes. The more adults are able to help children learn to draw the nourishment they need from these roots, the more they help them sit at the feet of Jesus, where all their feelings, needs, desires, longings, and hopes will find their ultimate resting place. The emotional health children gain comes from aligning themselves with the way God made their hearts to work best. In the next chapter, we'll explore the root that feeds all the other roots: feelings.

CHAPTER 10

Discipling the Emotions, Part 2: The Eight Feelings

Parents do well to give their children language for their emotions. In so doing, we provide our children with the tools Jesus had to express His own experience of life. Jesus felt sadness, loneliness, and gladness, among many other emotions. Living a fullhearted, God-honoring life demands that we have the words to communicate our experience of it as image bearers of the God who made our emotions.

The Eight Feelings[1] of the Spiritual Root System are hurt, lonely, sad, anger, fear, shame, guilt, and glad.

The most asked question about this system is "Why is only one feeling positive?" This is a great question. It's precisely this question that makes The Eight Feelings such a powerful tool. All these feelings are good, and each one is positive because of where it leads us:

---

1. "The Spiritual Root System."

- Hurt leads to healing.
- Loneliness moves us to intimacy.
- Sadness expresses value and honor.
- Anger hungers for life.
- Fear awakens us to danger and is the beginning of wisdom.
- Shame maintains humility and mercy.
- Guilt brings forgiveness.
- Gladness proves that our hopes are true.

However, each of these feelings can also become impaired, toxic, and unhealthy:

- Hurt can lead to resentment.
- Loneliness can become apathy.
- Sadness can express itself as self-pity.
- Anger can lead to pride and depression.
- Fear can lead to anxiety.
- Shame can turn into toxic shame and contempt.
- Guilt can lead to shamelessness.
- Gladness can become unrestrained pleasure without heart.

In recent years, our children's experience of life has become more tragic. Thanks to technology, kids are exposed to the fragility and brokenness of humanity at earlier ages with each passing year. For this reason, providing them with robust language to express and move through complex emotions is not just a nice skill to pass along; it's an essential kindness and a crucial way to bear the burdens of our children in love.

With a little coaching, we can help our children move from suppressing and denying their feelings to honoring their emotions as tools to help guide them through life with wisdom. Our feelings are like thirst—they are necessary bodily signals of needs, desires, longings, and hopes. Very few of us end up thirsty midway through the day and say, "Oh, I'm a terrible person because I need a glass of water."

But that is the experience many of us have with our hearts. We believe we are wrong for feeling angry or defective for feeling lonely. Yet as we will see, each of these eight emotions is good because they can lead us to the feet of Jesus. It is in the experience of these emotions that our children become covered in the dust of Jesus, as they learn to live fully.

Hurt

Hurt lets us know we have pain. Hurt tells us that we need something. It awakens us to our dependence on others and on God.

Without hurt, our bodies wouldn't know they need help. When we break a bone, we need to go to the doctor to get a cast and treatment. The same is true emotionally. If we feel betrayed, we need time and nurturing to heal. When a friend speaks harshly with us, it is right for us to feel hurt.

Our children may experience physical sensations of hurt, which are helpful to identify:

It was like a punch in my stomach.

It tore me in two.

I felt stabbed in the back.

Adults are often uncomfortable around hurt children, as they can become moody or withdrawn. But that discomfort only exacerbates an unhealthy response to hurt. Denial of hurt does not make it go away. Children can find temporary relief from hurt by numbing it with food, sports, video games, or any number of "fixes." But the very things they might use to numb or distract their hearts will only lead to more pain down the road. The fixes may allow them to survive, but they don't resolve their hurt. Even if video games temporarily remove the sting of hurt, the emotion of hurt is still holding the steering wheel of their heart.

But when our children learn to tell the truth about their hurt, others can help them heal. How might we help our children identify their hurts?

1. Name it for them.

"I can see that you're hurt" are some of the most empathetic words we can give our children. It frees them from the burden of knowing what they're feeling and gives them the freedom to simply say, "Yes, I am," and begin to receive help.

2. Notice their resentments.

Often, we begin to resent the people, places, and things that hurt us. Resentment, however, merely shifts the hurt we've received from others and asks us to carry it with us each day. It has the appearance of revenge, but in the end, resentment only amplifies the hurt.

3. Become aware of how your children answer your probing questions.

If "What's wrong?" is consistently answered with "Nothing," you ought to be suspicious that your child is nursing some hurt.

When our children are able to identify their hurt, they can step into an experience of healing. Simple acknowledgment of their wounds is the healthy response to hurt that leads them to recovery. This experience grows their faith because they see that God really does care about their hurt, as he also experienced hurt.[2] Children begin to learn that God can heal them in ways they cannot.

---

2. Mark 11:17; Matthew 26:67; 27:30; John 25:20.

Forgiveness must be a part of healing from hurt. We misunderstand forgiveness when we think it must lead to relational repair. Some hurt rightly severs relationships, and we do well to physically, emotionally, and even spiritually separate ourselves from those who do us harm. Forgiveness, rightly understood, involves seeing and acknowledging the extent of the harm someone has caused us and then releasing our right to resentment and revenge.

Here are some questions to discuss with your children around the emotion of hurt:[3]

1. What is one of your most painful memories?

2. Has anyone hurt you? Do you need to tell them?

3. How can I help you feel safe telling me about your hurt?

Lonely

God gave us the gift of loneliness to help us seek relationships. In Genesis 2, God saw, before the fall, that it was not good for man to be alone. Loneliness is our children's deep hunger to belong and be known by others. Often, children feel ashamed of their loneliness—as if it were a deficiency. But this could not be further from the truth.

Our children can be lonely for three things: themselves, others, and God.

Sometimes they may feel overwhelmed by life and disconnected from a true sense of rest. They may have not had a chance to simply *be* for quite some time

---

3. As we move through each of the eight emotions, I'll provide questions like those above. Parents, when you ask these questions of your children, try your best to listen, receive, and remain non-anxious. Do not try to fix them and resist the urge to explain their feelings away. Feelings are simply expressions of how we experience life. Just because you don't think your child should feel hurt, lonely, or sad doesn't mean they don't feel hurt, lonely, or sad. One surefire way to ensure your children will hesitate or resist sharing their feelings with you in the future is to try to fix them or explain away their feelings today.

with the incessant demands of school and other activities. Our kids desperately need a rhythm of work and rest to listen to their hearts and be renewed. Most often, this rhythm must be initiated by their parents.

Another expression of loneliness is our children's need for others. Especially as our children move into the later elementary years, their need for others matures. No longer are their relational needs met simply by being in the presence of others. Instead, they begin asking questions such as:

Will you be with me?

Will you listen to me?

Will you honor me?

While our children may live in the presence of many people, their loneliness will not be satisfied by numbers. Instead, loneliness will only be satisfied by depth.

A third type of loneliness is our emotional and spiritual longing for God. The paradox of our loneliness for God is that it will never be completely filled, answered, or quieted as long as we live. As I type this, just yesterday was the solar eclipse of 2024. People from all over the country traveled to the middle of the United States to witness a once-in-a-lifetime event. The entire eclipse lasted for three to four minutes. To be sure, it was spectacular and an incredible display of God's handiwork. But it only lasted three to four minutes. We long for experiences of God's greatness and will go through tremendous hardships to experience even moments of it.

The only solution to loneliness is intimacy. But without admitting loneliness, we will remain distant from God, others, and ourselves. Much of the lives we create for our children only hides their loneliness. We rush them around to events, activities, functions, and parties. We live lives of tremendous intensity but little relational depth.

Many parents are afraid of their children's loneliness because it reminds them of their own or perhaps signals that they haven't raised a child who will be voted "most likable" in the high school superlatives.

One of the most difficult experiences of my own life has been wrestling with the shame of my loneliness. I long for deeper relationships. I want to know myself better. I desire to know God in transcendent ways. But my experience of life constantly tells me to live in contempt of my desire for these relationships. Earlier today I desperately wanted to call one of my dear friends just to tell him, "I'm really lonely." However, I never made that call. Even with those closest to me, vulnerability seems too high of a hill to climb.

When our children learn to be ashamed of their loneliness, apathy sets in. Apathy denies our loneliness. Apathy says, "I don't care. It doesn't matter." The degree to which our children learn to put apathy in the place of loneliness is the degree to which they learn to place themselves as separate from humanity and God.

But when our children learn the gift of unashamed loneliness, they move to a place of health that pays dividends for the rest of their lives. How might we help our children take responsibility for their loneliness? These questions might move them in that direction:

1. I wonder if you're getting enough time to rest. Do you need us to adjust our family's schedule to allow you to get the time you need?

2. Which friends make you feel loved? What can we do to make sure you're able to spend the time you want with them?

3. What has amazed you about God this week? Where have you seen him at work? What do you long to know and learn about him?

As our children gain the ability to see and feel their loneliness and get what they need from relationships, they will become healthier people who enjoy the lives God has given them and humbly long for more.

Sad

Of all the emotions I have worked the hardest to repress, sadness is at the top. Sadness can feel uncomfortable because it reveals that we've lost something we value. Sadness gives us the gift of valuing and honoring life. In a nutshell, sadness is the emotion that tells us that life matters.

Many children hear some version of "Don't cry over spilled milk; pick yourself up, dust yourself off; you're fine." Adults say these things to children because sadness can be inconvenient. It takes emotional and physical space and time. Often a child's sadness feels irrational or disproportional to how we might feel in the same situation.

But this thinking misses the entire point. Our children are not adults. They are small, growing humans who become sad when they lose a stuffed animal or when a friend calls them "ugly." Adults reading this, listen up—what causes your child's sadness is completely irrelevant. Get the idea out of your head that some things are worth grieving and others are not. That is not your decision to make.

God invites adults to be a safe place for children to work through their sadness. In the presence of safe adults, children learn the mechanics of working through grief in a way that will build the resiliency to recover from their first breakup, first firing, and first experience with death. Processing their sadness over the loss of a stuffed animal is good, holy work and well worth your time and energy.

Sadness is a gift that opens us to healing. It helps us grieve. A denial of sadness does not make grief disappear. People often say of sadness, "That's just water under the bridge." But adults often awake to the realization that all the water has simply been collecting in their hearts. Unprocessed grief is a plague in adulthood. Sadness in adults comes out sideways in resentment, rage, and all manner of unhealthy expressions. Isn't that interesting? Some of the most hot-tempered people you know are likely the saddest people you know.

When our children do not learn to honor their sadness, two things typically develop as they learn to survive life: self-pity and denial.

Self-pity is a way to avoid sadness by asking others to feel our sadness for us. Children become masters at this skill when willing parents pacify sadness with concessions and enablement.

Denial sets in when sadness must be avoided. Without sadness, we cannot value life. Remember, sadness shows how much we value what was lost. But if I never truly love anything or anyone, then I don't have to feel sadness when loss comes. So, to avoid sadness, I'll simply stop ascribing value to things.

How can we help children grow in the ability to experience healthy sadness, which leads them to healing?

1. Honor their sadness.

No matter how insignificant it feels to you, listen to their grief. This childhood experience of grief is building in them the skills to walk through greater sadnesses later in life.

2. Let them see you grieve.

It shows them that life has value. Cry at their kindergarten graduation. Write them notes when you must be out of town. Help them see that sadness is a necessary, not inconvenient, part of life.

3. Pray with them in their sadness.

We do not have all the resources within us to move through grief. Not even close. We need the Good Shepherd to lead us through the valley of the shadow of death into green pastures.

Anger

Many of us grew up thinking of anger as an emotion to be avoided at all costs. In truth, anger is perhaps the most important of all our emotions. It is the first step toward honest living because it shows that life matters to us, that we care about people, places, and things. It reveals the commitments of our hearts and unearths our desires.

Now, when you think of an angry person, you may think of someone punching a hole through a wall or yelling uncontrollably. This is not anger but an impaired form of fear known as rage (more on that later). Instead, we need to give anger an updated identity in our vocabulary. Anger is the emotion that motivates us to pursue our needs, desires, longings, and hopes. Anger is the emotion of caring.

Anger enhances our relationships because through it, we allow ourselves to be known by others. Anger wants others to know what we are deeply passionate about. If you are in a relationship with someone experiencing healthy anger, you know they know you, and you know you know them. They bring their whole self to the table and invite you to do the same.

Anger is worth nurturing in our children because it is the feeling that allows them to care. The wherewithal to have compassion toward another finds its roots deep in the soil of anger. In discussing childhood, I often hear parents talk about their kids being "a lot of a lot." I would describe one of my daughters in this way. She feels deeply about a lot of things, *and* nobody makes me feel more cared for than her. Her love is enormous because God has given her anger—the emotion of caring.

Jesus turned over tables in the temple, defended women caught in sin, and loved little children in the face of Pharisees because of his anger. He showed the vulnerability of full passion and compassion, the desire to make what had become rotten pure again.

When children are denied the freedom to express their passions as felt in their anger, what often results is depression. Depression shoves anger right back into our hearts. When children become depressed, their hearts dim and sometimes stop working altogether. They can no longer deal with sadness or hurt because they lack the anger to access those feelings.

Here are some questions to help cultivate the gift of anger in your children:

1. What are you passionate about? What do you want to do to pursue your passions?

2. What do you want to be true about you in five years? How can I help you get there?

3. What do you want to change? About the world, our family, our city, our church?

4. How do you think God feels about the things you love?

Fear

Fear, like many of the eight feelings, brings us the gift of seeing our need for help. And yet there is almost no feeling the church runs from more quickly than that of fear. Campaigns of "faith over fear" are ubiquitous but about as far from the biblical message as possible. In fact, nearly the opposite is true. To admit fear is a tremendous step of faith.

However, children are told from an early age to silence their fears. Perhaps adults do not know how to handle their own fears, let alone their children's. Maybe we worry that fear will produce weak children. And yet you cannot outrun fear. You can only replace fear with shame: the feeling that there must be something wrong with you. But this does nothing to help and only harms children.

Fear, healthily expressed, is an emotion of humility. It admits that we lack the resources we need to face life alone. It pushes back on the false virtues of independence and self-sufficiency. Fear can help us depend on someone else for a skill we lack. It can lead us to build friendships and learn while collaborating with others.

Above all else, fear leads us to God. Psalm 111:10 famously says, "The fear of the LORD is the beginning of wisdom." Fear offers us the opportunity to trust God with our need for help if we allow it to lead us away from isolation and into vulnerability.

How is it that wisdom begins with fear, as Psalm 111 says? Fear awakens us to danger and is a primal reaction to physical, emotional, and spiritual threats. When children become uncomfortable, their bodies let them know. Their hearts may beat faster. Their palms may grow sweaty. These fear responses are gifts. By listening to our fear, we acknowledge our value, fragility, and finitude. We prevent harm to ourselves and others. As we do this, we develop wisdom.

But too often, adults try to squash the fears of children, especially when they do not fit our grown-up parameters of what is worthy of fear. Take, for instance, a child who is afraid of the dark. Their fear may seem unreasonable to you, but only because you're no longer five years old. You have been afforded a lifetime of exposure to darkness that has conditioned you to feel safe. Your five-year-old has not had the experience you've had.

Parents need to develop grace and kindness around their children's fears. If we don't and opt to squash or shame our children's fears by telling them to "get over it," we don't actually solve the problem. We only make it worse. The fear itself becomes something to fear because now it not only produces fear; it also brings with it a side dish of shame. But parents who can walk children through their fears, no matter how silly they may seem, help them rehearse the skills of valuing themselves and gaining wisdom.

Unfortunately, children who do not receive guidance on what to do with their fear often live with chronic anxiety and/or rage—either in childhood or adulthood. Anxiety is an attempt to control our future in order to prevent the recurrence of fear. In so doing, children create an endless cycle of anxiety: Their attempts to control their anxiety inevitably result in more anxiety because they never acquire enough control. Anxiety also fails to help us see that unpredictability and chaos are simply a part of ordinary life.

When fear becomes anxiety, we constantly scan our environments for threats. People become threats. Situations become threats. Risks most certainly become threats. Our bodies live in fight-or-flight mode. When we are in real physical danger, fight-or-flight is a tremendous tool of heightened awareness. However, fight-or-flight as a tool to address emotional and spiritual needs denies our hearts.

Rage is perhaps the most noticeable and disruptive of our attempts to suppress our fear. Children express rage when they are terrified of exposing their hearts. A child expressing rage may look like they're in pain, but instead, they are actively rejecting the sensation of pain. This rejection takes the form of sending the pain back into the world. Remember, simply telling children to not be afraid does not remove their fear. It simply means they will experience an impaired version of fear—anxiety or rage.

Many adults conflate the emotions of rage and anger. However, they are very different. Rage rejects the fear of having desire, while anger acknowledges the depth of our desire. Rage denies our humanity, while anger embraces our humanity and all its desires. Mistaking rage for anger creates conflictual parent-child relationships. Since we have all experienced the discomfort of someone experiencing rage, you may have anxiety about anyone expressing anger toward us. They can look similar, but it is critical to know the difference. Otherwise we will not be able to identify and respond helpfully to our children's emotions.

Adults can help children move from anxiety and rage to healthy fear by helping them accept that living life fully must involve hurt. Hurt is not the obstacle; it is a gift that moves us toward taking healthy risks. It allows our children to grow as people who face life on life's terms and tell the truth about their experience of it.

Fear is the beginning of wisdom. It is the admission of our need for God and others. When we confess our neediness, we find a God who is always in charge, powerful, caring, and able. This neediness grows our faith and develops certainty in the only one who will never fail us. This certainty is the antidote to our anxiety. This is a stunning paradox. We often don't want our children to be fearful because we are afraid of their worry. However, healthy fear is the solution to our worry.

Here are some ways parents can help children grow in their experience of fear:

1. Talk openly about the ways you need to grow. Children need to watch others acknowledge that they still need to grow.

2. When your children move into rage, remain non-anxious. Resist the urge to throw their rage back at them. Instead, remind them with your words and your body language that they are safe.

3. Take your children's fears seriously, no matter how small they are. Dialoguing with them about their fears helps them grow in wisdom. Ignoring or denying their fears only promotes shame.

Shame

We've commented on shame several times, but it's now time to dive a little deeper into this powerful and often hidden emotion. Healthy shame is the emotion that tells us, "I am limited. I need others. I need God. I cannot do this alone." It allows us to acknowledge and even expect that we will make mistakes.

In turn, it builds empathy for others because, after all, they are not that different from us.

The gift of shame is humility. In humility, our children learn that our gifts are not to be used to prove ourselves worthy but to serve others. Our children are humbled that God has made them like he has, both gifted and limited. Healthy expressions of shame help us give ourselves to something greater than ourselves. We need others, and others need us.

Healthy shame also helps us rightly see God's role in our lives. No longer are we held captive to doing everything right or needing to be in control. Instead, we can know God as the one who made all things and holds all things together for his glory and our delight.

Healthy shame gives value to our work. Our gifts come from God. We can do no good thing without his creative work in our lives, which gives meaning to everything we're able to do. Whether our children are learning in school, playing on the soccer field, or caring for a younger sibling, their activities and work have real meaning.

Shame, like many of the other emotions, helps us feel our incompleteness. We can recognize our gifts and be grateful for them while at the same time acknowledging our limitations. We are far from perfect. Instead, we are people capable of failure, harm, and great evil. When children understand healthy shame, it becomes easier for them to see their need for God and hope for the day when their shame will turn to glory.

Healthy shame also builds empathy in children. If our failures cause us pain, then we can see and honor the pain of others. We become compassionate people who know others will hurt us because we, too, hurt others. In that knowledge, we can forgive and extend grace instead of harboring resentment, thinking, *I would never do that.*

Impaired shame is quite another story. When healthy shame turns toxic, we equate humility with humiliation, failure with uselessness, and inability with worthlessness. Toxic shame tells us we are disqualified from relationships. Toxic shame makes us question, *Why would others want to be around me? Why would God want to know me?* In a very real sense, it is what Adam and Eve felt in the Garden of Eden.

The vast majority of the time, children receive the message of toxic shame from parents and influential adults. Many adults feel they must be hard on children to get them to succeed. We put immense pressure on children to achieve socially, academically, athletically, and even spiritually. Children often receive the message "To have value, I must perform." The saddest children I have ever known are those who not only experience toxic shame but feel it's simply the way that life is. They don't know any better, and nobody is there to help them find a better way.

Here are some ways parents can help cultivate healthy shame in their children:

1. Celebrate personality and character traits more than achievements. Resist the temptation to define your children by their usefulness.

2. Work to create sensible, reasonable, achievable goals for your children. Don't set the bar too high.

3. Remain connected to your children, especially in their failures, when they need to sense their value most tangibly.

4. Talk about your weaknesses. Don't allow your children to believe you have life all figured out.

Guilt

While shame is the feeling that recognizes our limitations and our capabilities to do harm, guilt is what we feel when we actually do something wrong.

Guilt tells me I have transgressed and need to work to repair and reconcile. Guilt tells me I need to ask for forgiveness.

Shame and guilt work together. The amount of forgiveness we experience is proportional to our willingness to express our shame and confess the full, transparent truth about the wrong we have done. Healthy guilt exposes our hearts in humility to others and God. What makes guilt so painful is that in asking for forgiveness, I am not only being completely honest about my failures, but I am also asking for a determination of the future of the relationship. What a risky, courageous act!

A common symptom of unresolved guilt is to receive forgiveness and yet persist in feelings of guilt. This is usually not guilt at all. Typically, this means we have moved into toxic shame, the feeling that we are defective and unforgivable.

Healthy guilt will always point us to relationships—we need to be reconciled to God, to others, and even to ourselves. Guilt is a gift that allows us to sustain life-giving relationships where we cannot help but hurt one another. It also deepens relationships as we expose our weaknesses and ask for and extend forgiveness.

When we can't experience healthy guilt, we seek to feel justified in our actions or provide explanations. In justification, we seek to deny responsibility: "I did the best I could." In providing explanations, we shift the blame for our actions: "If you had not done what you did, I would not have done what I did."

Justifications and explanations do not seek reconciliation. Instead, they are self-protective measures that keep others at arm's length and, in turn, keep us from what truly heals—relationships. When we constantly lean on statements such as "I did the best I could," we miss the point. What we need to accept about ourselves and others is that nobody has done their best. We are all in need of forgiveness.

Guilt can also be challenging for young children because they struggle to empathize with others. Remember, according to Piaget, before the age of seven, children are egocentric. They struggle to see the world through the eyes of others. Egocentrism makes it challenging for kids to see how their actions affect those around them.

Parents and adults in authority also have a tendency to punish children when they hurt others instead of moving them toward reconciliation. Punishment only teaches children how to feel the pain of unhealthy guilt and avoid future punishment; it does nothing to repair relationships, reconcile, and teach the skills to act differently next time.

But children who can learn to navigate their guilt to build, sustain, and deepen relationships with God, others, and themselves grow into resilient adults capable of bouncing back time and again from hardship. They grow through mistakes. They strengthen others by showing empathy in our shared stumbling through life.

So, how can we encourage children to move toward healthy expressions of guilt?

1. Ask for forgiveness from your children. Do it often and honestly. It is good for your heart and theirs.

2. Place relational reconciliation as the primary goal over and above punishment when kids disobey, break rules, or hurt others.

3. Prompt children to honor their guilt: "It sounds like you may need to ask for forgiveness."

4. Remind children of the gift of guilt. Their relationships will actually be strengthened by asking for forgiveness.

5. Resist demanding that children ask for forgiveness. This short-circuits their ownership of their feelings. Instead, help coach them through the process.

Glad

Those who pursue fullhearted living will know the joy of gladness. Gladness is the result of our willingness to feel the other seven feelings. Do not confuse gladness with happiness. Happiness is dictated by circumstances. If it is a sunny day outside, I may be happy. If it turns cloudy, I may feel less happy. However, gladness is about our capacity to walk through pain in pursuit of our needs, desires, longings, and hopes.

It's important to know, however, that gladness is not about outcomes. Sometimes we work really hard for something only to feel sad and hurt. But even in that, we can still be glad for the experience.

As I've mentioned before, I coach our boys' soccer teams every fall. Each year is different, with unique challenges, but I am always glad I spent the time out at the fields with them and their friends. Throughout the season, I experience hurt when parents are habitually late to pick their children up. I feel guilt when I put a player in a position where I know they may get hurt and they do. But I always walk away from a season feeling glad.

Likewise, our children may feel gladness when they work hard for something at school but come up short. Perhaps they had a big project they worked really hard on. Maybe they remembered to start working on it before the eve of its due date (a big win in and of itself!). Even with all their hard work, they still may only get a C+. They may not be happy with their grade, but they can feel glad that they worked hard and grew in ways that can't be communicated in a letter grade.

For our children to experience gladness, they must accept that they have very little control over their own lives. This seems to be the opposite of the message kids receive from the world today. Everywhere you look, kids hear grandiose messages proclaiming they can be and do whatever they set their minds to. This is simply not true. Gladness involves living in the tension that life is full of mystery, joy, confusion, elation, divisions, passions, and pains. When life is lived within this tension, we get the privilege of relying on God's sustaining grace.

Parents who shield their children from the full experience of life can do great harm to their children. I'm not saying you should expose your three-year-old to the full weight of life's tragedies. However, parents who prevent their children from experiencing pain and loss do not allow them to live life on life's terms. They deprive them of the full experience of gladness. Children who only experience the happy moments of life will learn to be temperamental. However, those who learn to trust God and lean on others in relationships will gain the sturdiness to live life and not simply survive it.

Sometimes families will try to manufacture gladness. We plan extravagant vacations and experiences to try to capture the heights of joy. For instance, we may watch a movie because we enjoy the entertainment and want to unwind and unplug for a bit. This is fine, of course, so long as we do not expect too much from the movie. When we acknowledge what a vacation or movie can and cannot give us, we move toward gladness. Vacations are never as good as we imagine they will be, and they end too soon, with the real world on the other side. Talking to your children about the gift and loss of a vacation provides a healthy framework for them to experience gladness without expecting too much from short-lived experiences.

Parents can help cultivate gladness in their children by doing the following:

1. Prepare them for painful situations instead of preventing exposure to pain.

2. Support them as they experience life in all its hurt, loneliness, anger, sadness, shame, guilt, and fear. Children who feel supported in walking through the other seven feelings will be more likely to feel the gladness of life.

3. Do not shy away from talking about hard things. Children experience a tremendous amount of sorrow. They will process the sorrow in either impaired or healthy ways. Not talking about hard things doesn't make them go away.

Concluding Thoughts

What I've just shared may feel like drinking from a fire hydrant. It's a lot for adults, let alone children. You may need some time to let it all sink in for you. You may also need to process what you're learning about discipling children in their emotions with a counselor. Children will rarely exceed their parent's emotional maturity. Recognizing your own emotional immaturity as an adult could be the greatest gift you could give yourself and your family.

In terms of actually using The Eight Feelings as a tool with children and families, here are a few tips.

1. Practice The Eight Feelings.

Practice identifying these emotions with your spouse, a friend, or a group of friends. As you become more fluent in the emotions, check in with one another frequently—even daily. The more repetitions you have with the language of The Eight Feelings, the more easily you'll be able to assess the condition of your heart and remain emotionally available and helpful to your children.

2. Don't tackle them all at once.

Talk about The Eight Feelings one at a time for as long as a week or month. Purchase a copy of *The Voice of the Heart* by Chip Dodd. It will provide you with much more information than I've provided here.

3. Make a chart of the emotions.

Display this list of emotions somewhere in your home. Do daily check-ins with your children and with yourself. At first, this will feel unnatural. Over time, you will find comfort in these moments of connection.

4. Notice Jesus.

As you read the Bible, notice when Jesus experiences the human emotions of shame, fear, or sadness. Help your children observe what he does with those feelings. Reflecting on how Jesus interacted with the world is formative.

Overall, my best counsel on discipling the emotions is to begin. Begin when it's hard. Begin when it's sloppy. Begin when you're not sure you're ready. God will meet you in your steps of faithfulness because he longs to form you and your children into beautiful images of God, capable of living in this world but longing for the world to come.

CHAPTER 11

Discipling Alongside the Church

I love to run. It is my favorite form of exercise, relaxation, and stress relief. At the age of forty, I dress much more modestly for my runs than I did at the age of twenty-seven, which is when a nasty rumor circulated within our church.

I used to be one of those crazy runners who would wear the absolute shortest shorts I could find. In the hot Alabama summers, I would also drop the shirt so as to reduce the risk of heat exhaustion (and, if I'm honest, work on my tan). The kids in our ministry grew fascinated by my exercise routine, as they often saw me out running in our small town.

One day, a child in our ministry, Daniel, commented to his mother that he saw me run by their house in my underwear. When his mother insisted that this certainly wasn't true, Daniel doubled down, "No, Mom, Mr. Chris really was in his underwear!" Apparently I ran past their house again a few minutes later. Daniel's mom confirmed what he saw—Mr. Chris was, to her proper, Southern eyes, indeed running in his underwear. I like to think of it as confirmation bias.

To be clear, I was not in my underwear. However, I'm sure my shorts were shorter than some mens' underwear. In our traditional Alabama town where 95 percent of men never exercise because they are too busy hunting and fishing, I was an understandably confusing anomaly.

The rumor mill churned at the church, and before long, another parent confronted me: "Are you really running through town in your underwear?" I burst out laughing. What began as a five-year-old's confusion erupted into a white-hot rumor of public indecency by the children's pastor! Thankfully, after a few conversations, the rumor was put to rest.

Ahhh, the church…the beautiful, challenging, wonderful, hurtful rumor mill that has saved me and others from landing our lives in a ditch more times than I can count. If you spend enough time around a church, you, too, can have your own rumor mill stories. God's people hurt one another, gossip, and believe the worst. But (and that's a big *but!*) it's also the place God has promised to work.

You will experience hurt from the church. Some of it will be humorous, like my running story, and some of it will be quite painful. It's an unfortunate reality of living life side-by-side with other saints. But, if you look for it, you will also find God at work. In healthy churches, you'll find those who will listen and pray with and for you; you'll find the word of God preached and the sacraments celebrated. You'll find companions for the journey and mentors who have gone before you. You may even find those who need your guidance.

The church belongs to Jesus and is the community he planned for his people's protection and growth. He tells his disciples that the gates of hell will not prevail against the church and that the keys of the kingdom belong to it.[1] In other words, the church is the place where the kingdom of God is enacted on earth.

---

1. Matthew 16:18–19.

The church is where God's people visibly place themselves under God's authority.[2] In the church, the wisdom of God is revealed to his people.[3] It is the place we find restoration when we have fallen into sin.[4] In the church, we live out the Great Commission to make disciples, and it is where Christ shows himself to be preeminent above all things.[5]

Over the years, I've known families who long to follow Jesus but are suspicious of the church. It never goes well. Just as you can't have me over for dinner without my wife, Sarah, you can't have Jesus without his bride.[6]

I've also known plenty of families who left the church for one reason or another. I can't think of one success story from these families. The decision to leave may not be met with consequences in the short term, but in the long term, the fruit of this decision is destructive.

If you want to raise a child to be a disciple of Christ, the church is where they become covered in the dust of Jesus, and it begins before they can even walk. In our church, when a family welcomes a child (through birth or adoption), we hold a celebration. Central to the celebration is the pastor's encouragement to the parents. It always includes some formulation of these elements:[7]

- That they teach the child to read the word of God

- That they instruct him or her in the principles of our holy religion, as contained in the Scriptures of the Old and New Testaments, an excellent summary of which we have in the Confession of Faith, and in the Larger and Shorter Catechisms of the Westminster

---

2. Ephesians 1:22; 5:24.
3. Ephesians 3:10.
4. Matthew 18:15–20; Galatians 6:1.
5. Acts 2:11; Colossians 1:18.
6. Ephesians 5:24–32.
7. "The Book of Church Order of the Presbyterian Church in America," section 56.4, Office of the Stated Clerk of the General Assembly of the Presbyterian Church in America, 2022, https://www.pcaac.org/wp-content/uploads/2022/09/Website-BCO-2022-Full-Book-WITH-BOOKMARKS.pdf.

Assembly, which are to be recommended to them as adopted by the Church, for their direction and assistance, in the discharge of this important duty

- That they pray with and for their child
- That they set an example of piety and godliness before him or her and endeavor, by all the means of God's appointment, to bring up their child in the nurture and admonition of the Lord

The parents then take a series of vows:[8]

> **Do you acknowledge** your child's need of the cleansing blood of Jesus Christ, and the renewing grace of the Holy Spirit?
>
> **Do you claim** God's covenant promises on their behalf, and do you look in faith to the Lord Jesus Christ for their salvation, as you do for your own?
>
> **Do you now unreservedly dedicate** your child to God, and promise, in humble reliance upon divine grace, that you will endeavor to set before them a godly example, that you will pray with and for them, that you will teach them the doctrines of our holy religion, and that you will strive, by all the means of God's appointment, to bring them up in the nurture and admonition of the Lord?

I list all of these to show the great deal of intentionality behind this celebration. This time is not a glorified photo op draped in Bible verses. It's a solemn

---

8. "The Book of Church Order," section 56.5.

moment where each family makes promises to God before the entire church, not in a private ceremony. Many have likened it to the seriousness of a wedding, and I think that is right in many ways.

The church gathers for this as witnesses but also because they have a vow to take as well. Whenever I have the pleasure of leading one of these times, I assure those gathered that the child is too young to understand or even remember what's going on. The congregation takes this vow for the benefit of the parents. For that reason, I encourage the church to respond *loudly* so as to create a concrete memory the parents can recall when hard days come, when they need their friends, and when they need to lean on the church for help. The question reads,

> **Do you as a congregation undertake** the responsibility of assisting the parents in the Christian nurture of this child?[9]

Imagine the roar of 100, 200, even 500 or more voices in robust unison, saying, "*We do!*"

These celebrations remain one of my favorite practices of the church—promising to support one another in the ambitious work of raising a human. To acknowledge that this child will need far more than their parents can provide is a sobering admission of our neediness and a recalibration of our exceptions to what biblical discipleship looks like. Parents essentially vow that they cannot be the sole disciple-makers of their children. Instead, we humbly put ourselves under the discipleship of Jesus. It is beautiful on every level. It is one of those rare moments in life that make you feel truly seen.

The Centrality of the Church

The church is the community of God's people. Nobody should try to "go it

---

9. "The Book of Church Order," section 56.5.

alone," attempting to follow Jesus in isolation. As messy, broken, and dysfunctional as the church can be, it is worth fighting for. After all, Jesus did not give his life as a ransom for entrepreneurial, solo, pioneering Christians. Instead, he loved the *church* so much that he called her his bride. He loved his bride so much that he died for her.[10]

However, the current trends for our children's generation are bleak. For the first time in eighty years, church membership fell below 50 percent in 2020.[11] From World War II through the mid-1990s, church membership among adults was almost always at or above 70 percent.[12] Thousands more churches today are closing than starting.[13]

I can remember sitting in a Modern European History class my freshman year of college. The professor presented statistic after statistic about the decline of the European church amid the rise of cultural liberalism. He made the bold statement, in 2002, that "this will be the US in twenty years." I dismissed him at the time, but now this reality is coming to pass before our eyes.

For the first time in our lifetime, our children will encounter a society where the cultural scales have tipped. It is no longer culturally acceptable to attend a church. If you do, you are in the minority. For many, the church is seen as regressive and obsolete.

What do our children need from us at this moment? Here are a few thoughts from my experience as a pastor.

1. They need to know *why*.

They need to know the *why* for their *what*. Gone are the days of telling

---

10. Ephesians 5:25.
11. Jeffrey M. Jones, "U.S. Church Membership Falls Below Majority for First Time," Gallup, March 29, 2021, https://news.gallip.com/poll/341963/church-membership-falls-below-majority-first-time.aspx.
12. Jim Davis and Michael Graham, *The Great Dechurching* (Zondervan), 2023, 11.
13. Aaron Earls, "Protestant Church Closures Outpace Openings in U.S.," Lifeway Research, May 25, 2021, https://research.lifeway.com/2021/05/25/protestant-church-closures-outpace-openings-in-u-s/.

people they should come to church simply because they should. This next generation is not duty bound like yours may have been. This messaging needs to begin early. We cannot wait until high school to connect the dots for our youngest church members. Parents, teachers, and church leaders need to think well about exactly why church is critical to the lives of children. Between the ages of four to fourteen, children form their core identities. To begin spiritual formation at the tail end of this spectrum or even after is a great disservice.

2. They need to know it's worth it.

Our children need the adults in their lives to provide a compelling reason for why following Jesus is worth it. They need to hear a chorus of adults, not simply their parents, speak openly about their faith and why it is of central importance to their lives.

3. They need to know it's for you…and them.

Parents need deeper and deeper understandings of grace for their own lives. We need to stop thinking of church as a place where we "pass down the faith" to a younger generation. Go to a bank and start a trust fund if you want to "pass things down" to your children. Parents, follow Jesus simply because *you* need what only Jesus can provide. The moment parents stop being moved and compelled by the gospel is the moment we begin to look like frauds to our children's watching eyes. They do not need a set of core beliefs handed to them. They need to see real faith in action. Only then will they want it for themselves.

The Importance of Church Membership

Becoming a church member means leaving behind the comfort of individualism and voluntarily binding yourself to others. It is a beautiful picture of the gospel—people from all walks of life mutually submitting to one another and to God.[14] We become members of a local church because Jesus joyfully left behind his comfort and bound himself to us.[15] We do not belong to ourselves. We belong to God and to others, and what we do in joining a church bears witness to the beauty of Jesus and his kingdom. And don't miss this: Church membership is as important for your children as it is for adults.

For some, membership may seem like an unnecessary hurdle for otherwise committed church attenders. After all, the Bible is relatively silent on the matter. However, there are several ways we can infer that membership is vital to the life of your family and your church:

1. Church membership is implied in the way the New Testament requires elders to care for the flock in their charge. How can the elders know who is in their care if there is not the reciprocal action of joining the church as a member?[16]

2. Church membership is implied in the metaphor of the body of Christ.[17]

3. Church membership is implied by the way the church is to discipline its members. The church is the final court of appeal in matters of church authority as it relates to membership.[18]

4. Church membership is implied in the biblical requirement of all Christians to be submitted to a group of church leaders, elders, or pastors. The New Testament commands individuals to submit to a specific group of leaders.[19]

---

14. Ephesians 4:16; 5:21.
15. Philippians 2:5–8.
16. Acts 20:28.
17. 1 Corinthians 12:21–26.
18. Matthew 18:15–17.
19. Hebrews 13:17.

Church Membership and Children

Many faithful churches use the process of children's membership as an opportunity for intensive discipleship. In our church, for example, we walk children and their parents through sessions called (1) "The Gospel as the Story of the Bible," (2) "Baptism," (3) "The Lord's Supper," and (4) "Why the Church Exists." We begin these sessions after a parent has indicated that they believe their child has come to saving faith in Jesus.

After these sessions, each family receives homework to complete alongside their children as a follow-up. We call this packet of homework the Funbook (because who likes a *work*book, anyway!).

After they complete their Funbook, each child has an individual meeting with an elder in our church where they're able to share what Jesus has done in their lives and what they love about God. During this time, they are also able to ask questions and get to know one another.

At the end of this meeting, which at least one parent must sit in on, the elder asks the parent, "How have you seen Jesus at work in your child's life?" What an amazing time to affirm the work of God in the life of your child! Young adults who were children in my ministry years ago still remark at the significance of these meetings on their walks with God.

Within a few weeks of meeting with an elder, children stand before the church and take these vows:[20]

> **Do you acknowledge** yourself to be a sinner in the sight of God, justly deserving his displeasure, and without hope save [except] in his sovereign mercy?
>
> **Do you believe** in the Lord Jesus Christ as the Son of God,

---

20. "The Book of Church Order," section 57.5.

and Savior of sinners, and do you receive and rest upon him alone for salvation as he is offered in the gospel?

Do you now resolve and promise, in humble reliance upon the grace of the Holy Spirit, that you will endeavor to live as becomes the followers of Christ?

Do you promise to support the church in its worship and work to the best of your ability?

Do you submit yourself to the government and discipline of the church, and promise to study its purity and peace?

As you can tell, our process by which children join our church is robust and thorough. I've provided it for you in some detail as an outline for your church should yours not already have such a process. But I've also included it in this book for a more important reason.

Church membership for children is much more than a formality or jumping through hoops. For churches that take discipleship seriously, it is an important part of their plan to teach your children the doctrines of our faith. It is, therefore, well worth the time and effort it takes.

Trends

Having been in children's ministry since before the smartphone, I have witnessed a great deal of disturbing trends among Christian parents. At the beginning of my ministry career, I could count on Sunday. All day. Families had nothing going on after church until bedtime. No sports leagues were allowed to hold practices, and no schools could hold functions (I did minister in the Deep South during that time).

However, as the years progressed, things changed quickly. First, it was Wednesday evenings (the other night of the week held as a quasi-sacred space for church activities). Wednesdays evaporated from the calendar as our town grew and overcrowded recreational field access didn't. Then, it was Sunday evenings…seven-year-old baseball teams hosted practices at the field right next to the church *while we held a discipleship program for children at the church.* The straw that broke the camel's back for me was when one of our key children's ministry volunteers became the coach of one of these Sunday evening teams.

Next was early Sunday afternoon. Kids came to church dressed for any manner of dance lesson or football practice. If the sermon went too long, parents would just get up and leave so they wouldn't miss the warm-up.

Then came the day I thought I'd never see. Maybe I was naive. Sunday mornings. Practices, tournaments, games, and rehearsals laid right over the top of Sunday morning without a second thought. Our church had elders (*elders!*) taking groups of children to baseball tournaments two to three weekends each month. The joke in our football-frenzied university town was that college football got the fall through mid-January (especially if we made the national championship), the Nutcracker got all the little girls in December, and youth baseball got all the little boys from March to June. So, if you wanted to do anything of significance as a church, it had to occur in a six-week window between the middle of January and February.

This is insanity. Your child is not going to be a professional baseball player.

But they learn so much from being a part of a team.

True…and that's why they need to come to church. They'll learn even more from being a part of a family.

But they have more fun at dance than church.

I don't doubt that. I wish I could grow into a healthy adult while eating Snickers bars all day. That's not the way it works. I need to discover the goodness of eating food rich in value…even if I don't particularly like it at first. Besides that, fun happens when we reach a critical mass of kids. If we don't have your kids there, we will never have the numbers to have a lot of fun.

But we are so busy as a family during the week. If my child is going to play sports, it has to be on the weekend.

You will always, always, always make time for the things you value. It sounds like obedience to your career and your children's wants have superseded your desire for obedience to Christ.

But if my child is not on this particular team, they will be left out of a friend group.

They probably will, but they will be introduced to a whole new group of friends at church. Would you rather your child spend their formative years around others who prioritize following God or those who prioritize following their selfish ambitions?

If this dialogue feels confrontational, it is. The forces sucking kids away from churches are just as confrontational. The church of today needs strong leaders who can graciously but firmly call families back to sanity.

A Note from a Children's Pastor to Parents

I've interacted with my fair share of parents over the years, the majority of which have been supportive, kind, and my biggest cheerleaders. I've always felt appreciated, and for that I am thankful, but I know that is not the norm. Every week, I get messages from children's leaders across the world who are at their wits' end and want to quit.

The tenure for most in children's ministry is less than eighteen months. The burn-out rate is sky high, and we do very little in the way of apprenticing the next generation of leaders. And so, as winsomely and unwhiningly as possible, I want to lift the everyday church member's eyes to the reality their children's director/pastor meets with on a weekly basis. My hope is that this list will help you see your church leaders with eyes of compassion.

1. **Most children's leaders have little to no formal training in child development, the Bible, ministry, systems, teaching, or volunteer coordination.** The vast majority of those in children's leadership positions found their way there simply because they were willing to accept a role few wanted to take. Know this about your leaders, and come alongside them in the ways you are able.

2. **Because the average tenure of children's leaders is eighteen months, your children's director/pastor is likely young and/or inexperienced.** Remember that when you were twenty-five, you too had a lot of growing up to do.

3. **Running a children's ministry is like running a church within a church, only with less support and more high-maintenance congregants.** Your children's leader needs the willing support of parents, empty nesters, newlyweds, and grandparents. This work cannot be isolated to a few experts. Raising children is something the whole congregation vows to participate in. Children's ministry is a visible, tangible, and vital way you can uphold your vow and make a difference in the life of a child.

4. **Your children's leadership has very little time each week to effect change.** It is not fair to compare your child's development in a church program to, say, their math class at school. There is only so much any children's leader can do with two hours each week. Because of this, your children's ministry desperately needs your support at home. An hour or two of instructional time on Sunday does very little to move the needle of biblical literacy. Your

church is no replacement for leading your children to Jesus at home. Ask your children's leadership how you can support your children's learning at home. Children from families who are active in disciple-making stick out not just in their knowledge but also in their character and love for Jesus.

Concluding Thoughts

I once knew a family who drove an hour each way to be a part of a church. Most of us do not need to do this to be a part of a gospel-rich, Bible-believing church, but they did so because of the rural nature of where they lived. Year after year, mile after mile. Three times per week. All told, they invested well over fifteen hours per week in their church community. It meant limiting their involvement in extracurricular activities. It meant the father turning down a promotion that would require more travel. Their faithfulness in the pursuit of God's means of grace both confounds me and inspires me.

My dad used to tell me that there are two truths to life: (1) You'll never have enough space because you'll always find stuff to fill it with. (2) You'll never have enough time because you'll always fill it with what's most important to you.

This family knew they had a finite amount of time in any given week. Therefore, if pursuing God was going to be their first priority, it had to be reflected in their schedule and their decisions.

As you lean into discipling your children, I hope and pray you will not have to drive an hour each way to find a good church. However, it is worth considering what changes will be required to meet your goals. If I want to improve my strength but never pick up a weight or do a push-up, I'll never get any stronger. Families who want to see their children grow in Jesus make concerted and sometimes challenging decisions.

CHAPTER 12

Discipling with a Plan

A week ago, we had a house guest. To be more specific, it was one of my co-workers with Kaleidoscope Kid's Bibles. She was coming to town for three days to help work on a special project that would have taken us three years over Zoom. Months before, I booked her flight and we'd put together some rough outlines of what we'd work on while she was in town. However, I'd neglected nearly every other detail.

One week from her arrival, my type A wife asked me all the planning questions. Where would she be staying? What were we going to eat? Did she have dietary restrictions? What does she like with her coffee in the morning? Would we need to work nights while she was there? Where would we work? Did you remember that our kids use the guest bathroom, and so we will have to move them out of the bathroom while she's here? Who is going to clean before and after she's here?

I had no answers. We'd just figure it out and "play things by ear." This, as I'd soon discover, was not the correct answer. I'd neglected all these details and more, which led to some, shall we say, friction between us.

Thankfully, we recovered, regrouped, and formed a plan to help the week run smoothly. At the age of forty, I relearned a lesson I've already relearned many times before: If you're going to do something well, you better have a plan before you start. Desires without plans create anxiety. Anxiety leads to either fight or flight. We either double down to force something to work, or we run from the desire altogether because it's proven too difficult. It is for this reason that I strongly suggest families develop a plan for discipleship that works for them.

Most plans are better than no plan at all, and there are many helpful tools out there to help families plan for discipleship. What I've outlined on the next few pages is simply a process I've walked many families through. It's a bit organic, perhaps even a bit rough for some. But I humbly offer it because it's an amalgamation of what's worked for me and many other families.

Step 1: Observe Your Family

I've had more anxiety-filled conversations with first-year parents than I care to remember. "Billy is three months old, what should we do for discipleship? I really feel like we're behind." This sounds funny, but I can't tell you how many interactions I've had with parents of children under the age of one who already think the ship has already sailed on discipleship. Here's the truth: If I give a parent of a three-month-old one more thing to do other than keep the child alive and stay married, I'd probably commit pastoral malpractice.

Observing your family is an exercise in watching reality. Too often, our plans for discipleship are made in some abstract universe divorced from real life. Frequently, our plans are made in an effort to keep up with the family we see on social media (who also has a perfectly decorated home, detailed meal plan, and a mom who somehow manages to wear makeup and a new dress every day to simply be at home).

Observing your family is taking the time to honestly take stock of the context, patterns, and habits already at play in your home—some conscious and some subconscious. You might really want to have nightly family devotions, but you've never even had one. You may want to have a daily family prayer time, but you're only ever all home together when everyone's asleep.

You have the freedom to pursue discipleship in the ways that make sense for your family. You're free to revisit the commitments you've made in light of changing circumstances. You're free to ease into a routine when you are starting at zero.

It may be helpful for you to sit with a close friend or member of your extended family. Tell them about your desire to make a plan to disciple your children. Show them your schedule. Invite them to speak into your life. Remain open-minded with their feedback. They might tell you difficult things.

Another helpful practice is a SWOT analysis. You may be familiar with this tool, which stands for Strengths, Weaknesses, Opportunities, and Threats. Here's a copy of one I worked through with a friend recently as we observed his family together:

> **Strengths:** Their children are relatively close in age (seven and nine). Both children can read with some proficiency. The family already has a predictable routine from 6:00 to 8:00 each evening (dinner, dishes, bath, story time, and bed).
>
> **Weaknesses:** There is no family phone policy (for example, phones away during dinner). There's currently no formal discipleship in place (we're starting from scratch).
>
> **Opportunities:** Everyone tends to get up early, and nobody

has to be anywhere before 8:30 most mornings of the week. Their church offers resources for at-home discipleship. The kids have shown interest in learning about Jesus.

Threats: The children have soccer practice from 4:30 to 6:00 p.m. on Tuesdays and Thursdays. Everyone usually comes home tired, and the next morning can be a challenging start. Mom and Dad are not in a great routine of being discipled themselves.

However you choose to engage, this reflective process is a step in the right direction for any family. You can't build something until you know what the foundation looks like.

Step 2: Define Your Goals

While we don't want this to become overly cumbersome, I'm increasingly convinced that naming goals is helpful for almost any process. If you don't know where you want to get to, you'll have a hard time making a plan.

Recently, we redesigned our company's website. At the outset, we defined a few goals of the project: easier user experience, a more aesthetically pleasing layout, and a more efficient back end for our team. We spent hundreds of hours on this project and would have traveled down far too many rabbit trails if we did not have these three goals as our guiding light. Anytime we were tempted to get distracted, we reminded ourselves of the narrowly defined set of goals we made at the outset. Focused goal-setting is a key to success for almost any system.

Let's return to my friend, the one with the boys ages seven and nine. We moved from the reflective exercise of observing his family to defining the goals he and his wife wanted for their family's discipleship. While they were tempted to list many, I encouraged them to stick to three. You can always add complexity to a simple system, but it is nearly impossible to bring simplicity to a complex system. Together, they wrote these three goals:

1. Cultivate our love for God's word.

2. Grow our love for our neighbors.

3. Build wisdom in our children.

While these goals are a bit on the broad side, they are a fantastic starting point to move to the next step.

Step 3: Make a Plan

With steps 1 and 2 complete, you can now make an informed plan to guide your family's discipleship. As you build your plan, especially if you are starting from zero, know that habits take time to form and habits take time to break. Remember this truth: Your family is currently achieving exactly the outcomes it was designed to produce. So if you are currently achieving zero at-home discipleship, your family system is designed to achieve that goal. Making changes and setting new patterns will not happen overnight and may take some time. Give yourself grace. Don't be overly rigid. Trees, bridges, and even buildings are designed to flex under stress from wind and earthquakes. Similarly, your family's plan must have some wiggle room to accommodate the ups and downs of life, or it will break under stress.

My friends came up with the following system to help guide their family. Again, notice how simple it is.

1. We will reduce the boys' soccer schedule to one season each year. No more year-round soccer for now.

2. Monday, Tuesday, Thursday, and Friday mornings from 8:00 to 8:15 is our family Bible time. We will aim for four mornings each week but give ourselves permission to begin with one morning each week and add a day each week until we reach four. In order to make sure we have extra time in the morning, we will pack lunches for school the night before and encourage the boys to lay out clothes for the next day before going to sleep. We'll start with reading through the Gospel of John.

3. One day each month, we will look for a way to love our neighbors. This may be having a family over for dinner, helping our elderly neighbor with some projects around her house, or having a night when the boys can invite a friend over for pizza and games.

4. We want to model wisdom for our children. This will look like us refraining from using our phones for social media and news scrolling until after they go to bed. We will also put screen-time limits on our family devices for the boys.

Simple, effective, achievable. This is a plan well designed for success, but it needs a few more things to give it staying power.

Community and Accountability

Your family cannot live in a vacuum. You are a part of a church community—a body where the parts mutually support one another. Few Christians really tap into the true power of living in community with other believers. In this last step, I encourage families to share their plan with another family. This is not a bragging session. If anything, it's an admission that you want to do better. This may feel vulnerable, perhaps a little too intimate for some of you. That's okay. Give it a chance. It will feel normal with time. Because by now you know I love steps, here's a simple guide to help you through this process.

1. Identify a family you feel safe sharing with.

This could be a contemporary but might also be someone younger or older than you. Ideally it should be someone trustworthy who will extend grace to you and hold your feet to the fire.

2. Invite the family over for dinner.

Share what you're doing as a family and why. Let the kids be involved in the conversation if it feels appropriate. Ask for feedback, counsel, and advice. Perhaps this will ignite change in your chosen family or prompt them to share their own discipleship journey with you.

3. Initiate a request for accountability.

The best forms of accountability are where the family asking for the accountability is the one active in reporting progress. Do not saddle someone else with the burden of remembering to ask you how you're doing. You are the one who checks in with them. The best forms of these that I've seen are over a group text where each family shares a weekly update on how things are going.

4. Pray.

If you've just walked through all the steps above, it may not seem world-changing, but it absolutely is. Generational change happens through seemingly small steps of faithfulness. For this reason, Satan wants nothing more than to distract, discourage, and destroy. Pray for the Spirit to lead your family in steadfastness when it would be easier to give up. But don't stop there. Pray for God to do a supernatural work in your family. Salvation and all its benefits are always a miraculous work of the Spirit.

See, that wasn't so scary after all. You can do this! Taking these first steps is half the battle. Your family can begin today, and it will completely change the trajectory of your life.

Discipling Without a Plan

You read that right. After you just read most of a chapter on planning, I'm now going to invite you to also engage in disciple-making without a plan...sort of.

Especially as children move into preadolescence and then again into the teenage years, parents need to gain ninja-like skills when it comes to discipleship. Opportunities to talk may become more infrequent. Many parents bemoan the fact that their teens only open up and talk after 11:00 at night. That sounds exhausting. But it also sounds like it requires the eyes to see and seize opportunities wherever they present themselves. In fact, it sounds like bearing the burden of adolescence as you once bore the burden of early childhood.

Think of how Jesus went about discipling his followers. He didn't have a precise plan (so far as we can tell) other than steadily making their way to Jerusalem for his death, burial, and resurrection. He was the master of discipling without a plan. Literally turn anywhere in the Gospels, and you'll find Jesus simply discipling his followers through their experiences of life. It must have been a roller coaster. One day you're watching pigs run off cliffs, and the next you're feeding thousands of people from a boy's Lunchable.

Our kids live lives of extraordinary complexity. They move at the speed of life, which is only getting faster by the day. Our attempt to minutely plan every family discipleship moment, as admirable as it may be, is not realistic. In fact, our rigid plans may be detrimental. Here are a few reasons why.

1. Real discipleship happens in real time.

Relegating discipleship to a defined time during the day is fine, but if discipleship is exclusive to that time, it feels fake, disconnected, and irrelevant. It's as if we exit real life, do discipleship, and then catch the next on-ramp back to real life. Narrowly defining discipleship as a specific time in a family's schedule is akin to disconnecting Sunday worship from the rest of our week.

2. We can meet them in their need (like God does).

Off-script discipleship allows us to meet our children where they are with particular encouragement when they need it most. You don't say, "You know, son, that's a great question. Let's discuss it at our next family discipleship meeting on Tuesday." No, you dig in with them at the moment of need, helping them connect to God in their times of celebration, trial, disappointment, and joy.

3. The unexpected moments may be the most life changing.

We become covered in the dust of Jesus at the most unexpected of times. Parents who know that God is their child's primary discipler remain curious about how God is at work. When the light bulbs go on, and the moment is right, great parents jump into action to usher their children where Jesus is already leading them. Just consider all the ways God was at work in unexpected ways and at unexpected times:

- Jairus didn't wish his daughter to be deathly ill, and yet Jesus met him in his moment of need.

- Nicodemus needed to meet with Jesus in the middle of the night.

- Zachaeus met with Jesus from the top of a tree.

- The woman at the well was just going to gather water at midday when she met Jesus.

- The dying thief met Jesus on the cross, moments before his death.

- Saul met Jesus on his way to murder Christians.

- And a group of fishermen met Jesus while they were tending their nets.

Concluding Thoughts

As we come to a close, I want to leave you with a few encouragements as a review of sorts from what we've learned together. If you take nothing else away from this book, remember this…

1. **You are the person for the job.** Before he created the world, God knew you would be your child's parent. He didn't make a mistake.

2. **You are not the sole discipler of your child.** Release yourself from that burden, and lead your children to Jesus. He cares for them far more and better than you. He is the only one who can bring your children to God.

3. **Jesus disciples your children moment by moment, not in disconnected moments.** Your children are always being covered in the dust of their rabbi as they follow Jesus, even when it might not be readily apparent to you.

4. **You need Jesus as much as your children do.** Do not neglect following Jesus in this intense season of raising disciples.

5. **God delights in you.** He delights in your children. His primary posture is one of love. He calls believers "saints" and not "sinners." We get the privilege of taking on the mind of Christ when we believe this.

6. **Remain curious about your children's behavior.** Learn from Jesus the patience, kindness, and gentle restoration your children need.

7. **Your children were created with bodies.** Increasingly, they live in a world that both devalues and overvalues the body. Encourage them to use their bodies to enjoy the world God created.

8. **Respect and respond to your children's unique developmental level.** They lack the experiences, skills, and knowledge you possess. This is not a liability; rather, it is an opportunity to bear their burdens in love.

9. **Your children are whole, connected, growing people.** They have feelings, needs, desires, longings, and hopes. Treat them with all the respect, kindness, and gentleness Jesus affords them.

10. **Humbly submit to a plan for discipleship,** connected with your local church and in vulnerable relationships with other believers.

I'm proud of you. I'm cheering you on. I believe, through the goodness of Jesus, that you can raise disciples at home.

Acknowledgments

Much of the wisdom of this book has come from conversations, encouragements, and experiences with people I love.

To my love, Sarah. Our life together is the backdrop against which all of God's goodness shines the brightest. Thank you for your generous love for the readers of this book, most of whom you will never meet. They will never know the hundreds of hours of time with me you willingly gave up so this work could come to fruition.

To my children: Jake, Caleb, Kate, and Charlotte. You are God's delight. Thank you for loving me despite all the ways I fail to live up to the aspirations expressed in this book.

To Jenny Floyd. Thank you for being the best teammate I could ask for. This book would have come to be with you alongside me, or I would have had a mental breakdown. I'm thankful it was the former.

To Jason Walch. You showed me that men can be Children's Pastors and that it can be really, really, really fun.

To Dick Cain. I would not be in children's ministry had I not seen so much of Jesus in you.

To Stephen, Stewart, Pace, and Charles. You helped me find my heart.

To Richard Vise. You told me I should write books, and I believed you.

To Grace+Peace Church in Chattanooga. You have been a beautifully imperfect embodiment of Jesus during the season I needed it the most.

To Benjie and Natalie Slaton. It is profoundly kind of Jesus to allow our family to do life and ministry alongside you. Thank you for believing in our vision of children's ministry, providing the space and time for creativity, and for your life-giving friendship.

To Andrew Wolgemuth and the team at Wolgemuth & Wilson. You believed I had something valuable to say when I wasn't sure I did.

To Kyle Hatfield, Heidi Picinic, and the team at Harvest House. Thank you for your trust and unwavering support. What you do for God's kingdom is nothing short of remarkable.

Chris Ammen is a children's pastor, writer, former educator, and the parent of four children. He is also the founder of Kaleidoscope, a company that specializes in creating beautifully designed retellings of every book of the Bible for older elementary school children (ages 7 to 11). Chris and his family live in Tennessee.